FUNKO STYLE

Blackheroes

in reverse

belongs to:

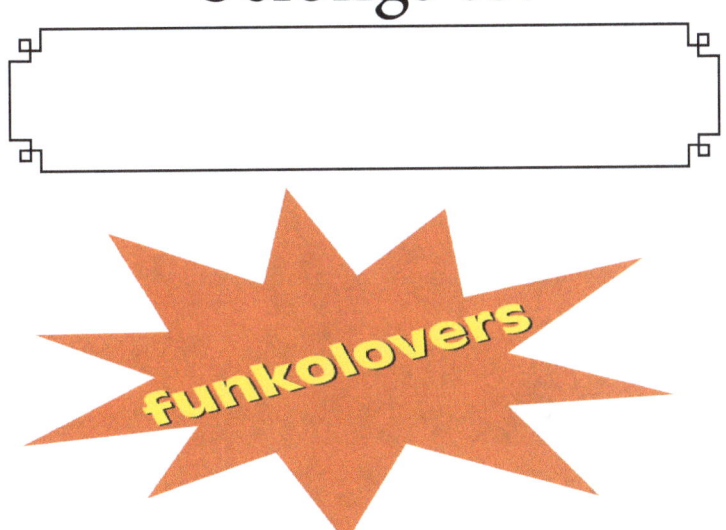

funkolovers

REGULAR PRACTICE IS KEY TO IMPROVING YOUR SKILLS

Recommendations:

1. Try to keep your wrist steady and stable as you draw to produce crisp, precise strokes.
Practice rotating your wrist to create smoother curves.

2. Draw crosshatching lines over an area can create interesting texture and add dimension to a drawing.

3. Apply different levels of pressure to the tracing to produce different tones and textures.

4. Add shadows and highlights to create depth and dimension. Adding shadows and highlights to a drawing can make it appear more realistic and three-dimensional.
Learn to use light and shadow to create effects of depth and to make objects appear bulkier.

5. If you need to make corrections, do so. Use an eraser to remove unwanted strokes; or correction pencil, as needed.

INSTRUCTIONS

Draw Funko-style blackheroes following these patterns with low opacity.
Trace the lines over the pattern and coloring it, you can change the colors or fills if you prefer.
Patterns have no background, so you can make the dystopian background, to your liking.

MATERIALS

Pencils, pens, markers, nibs, highlighters, eraser,
correction pencil, rules, and others that you prefer.

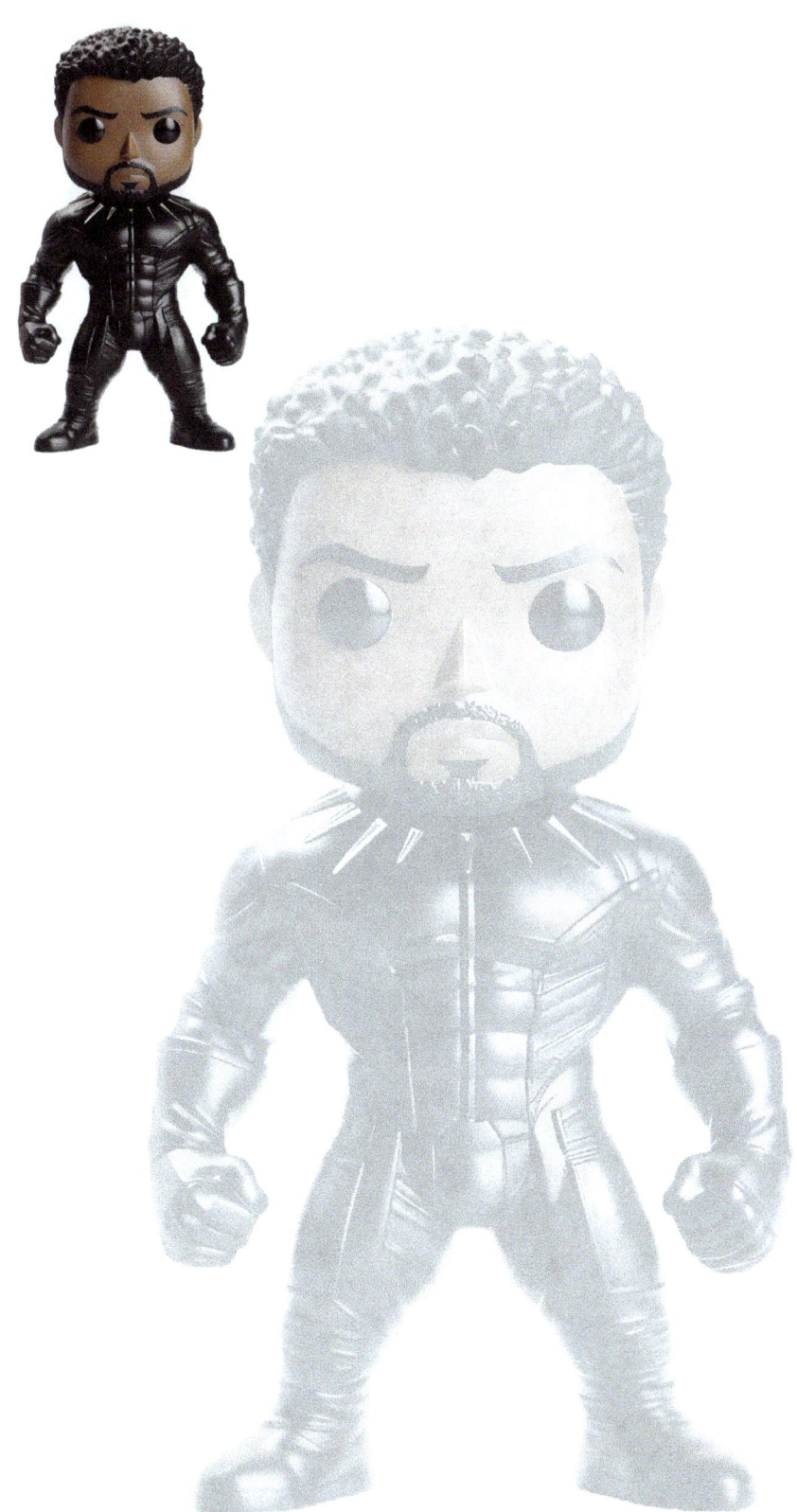

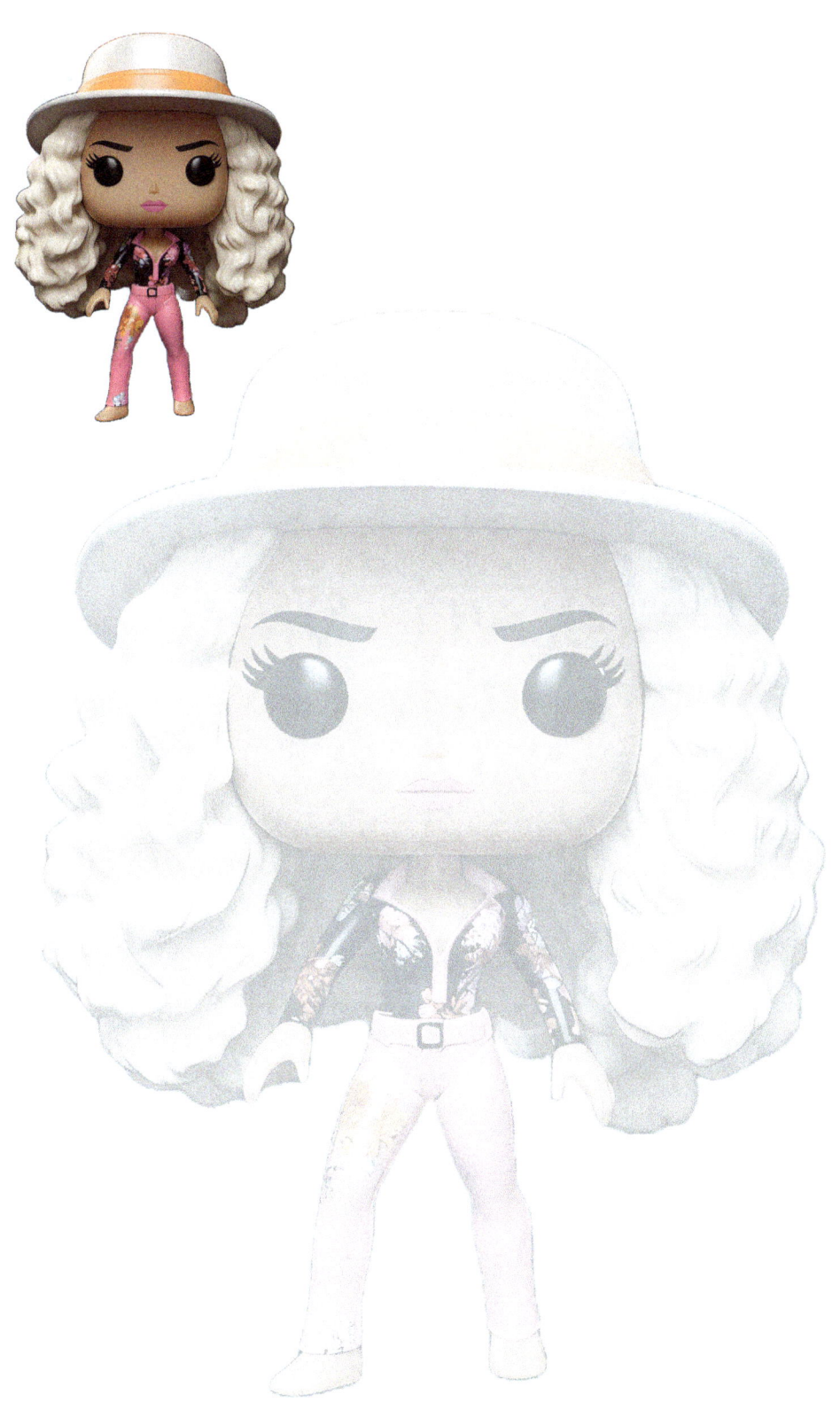

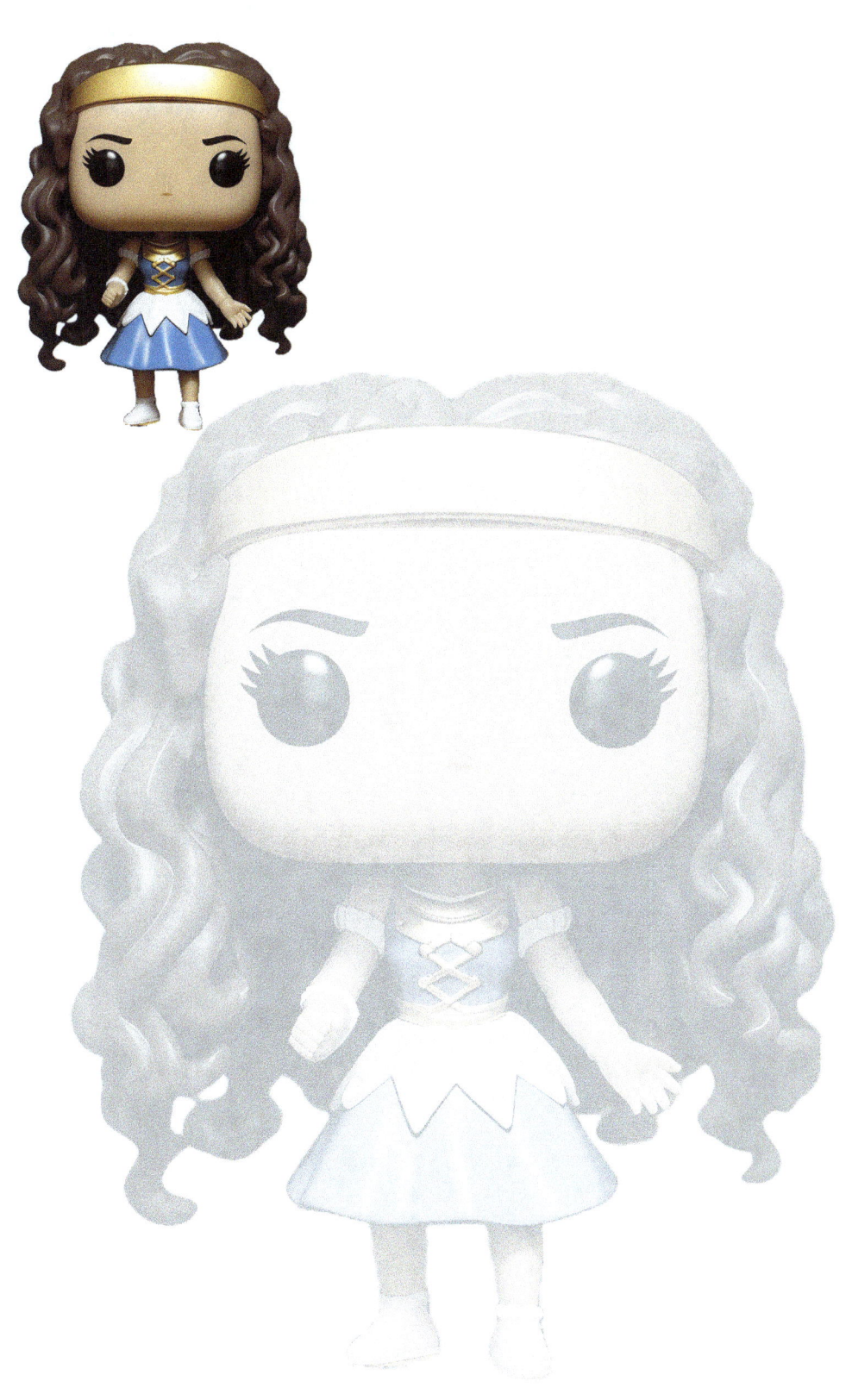

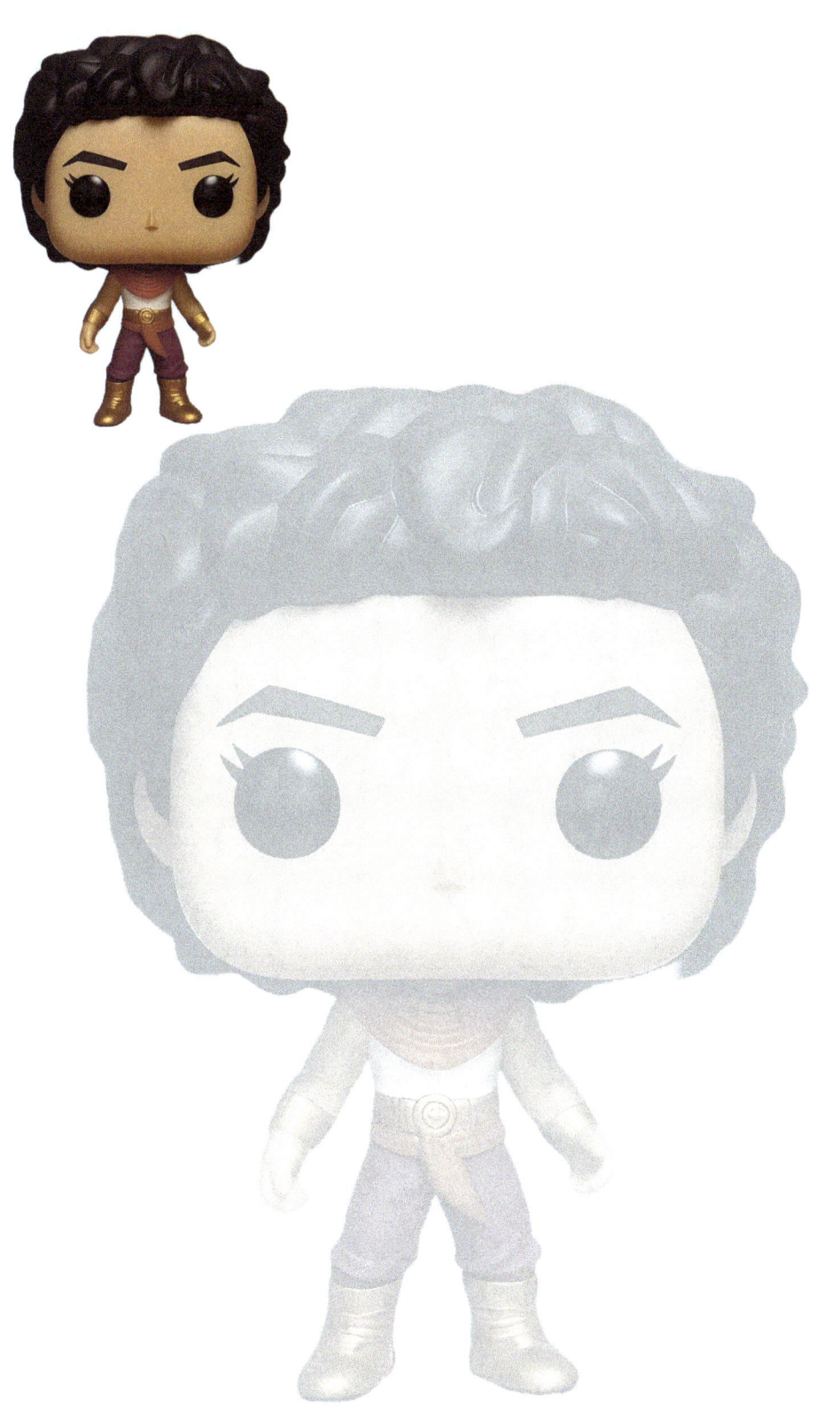

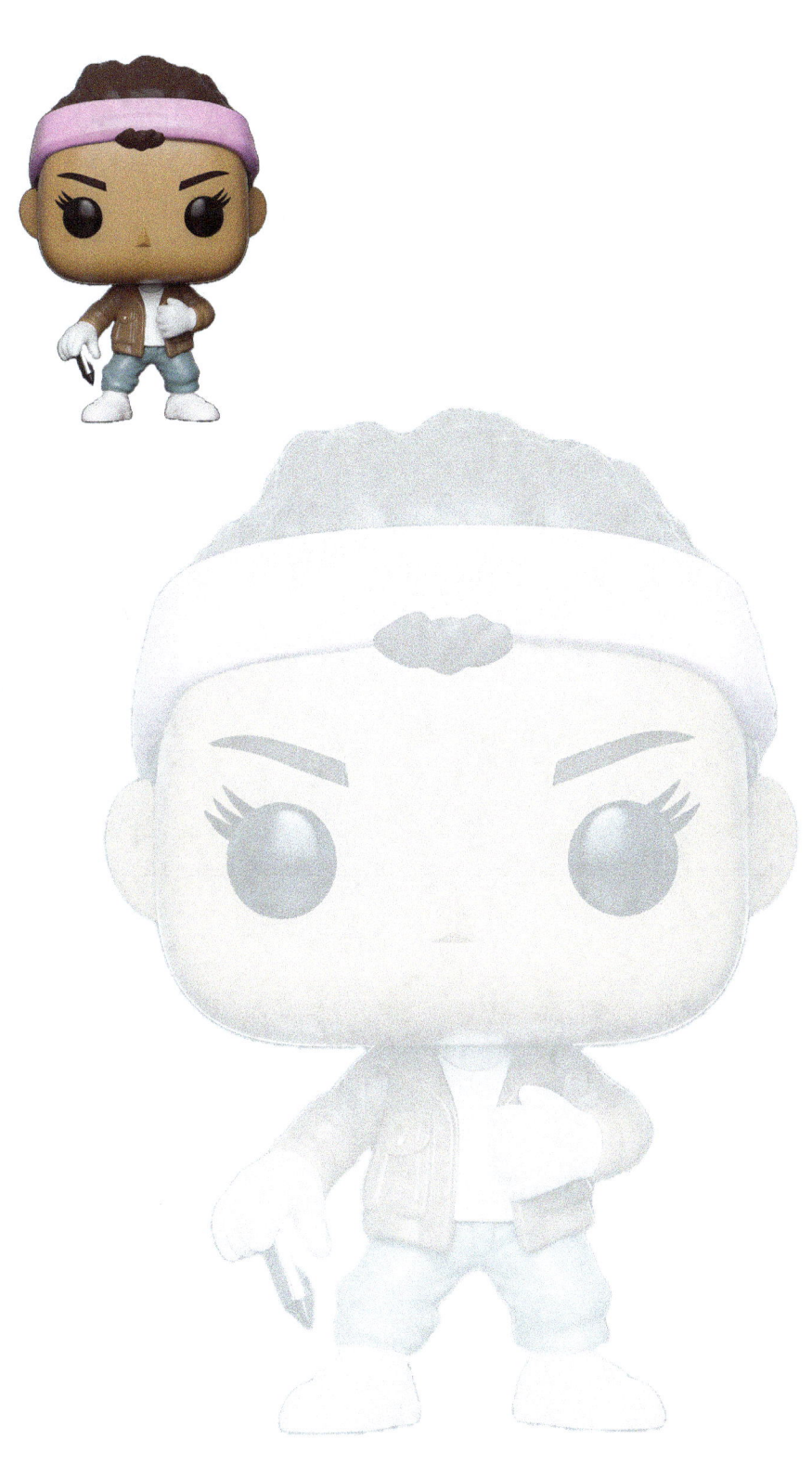

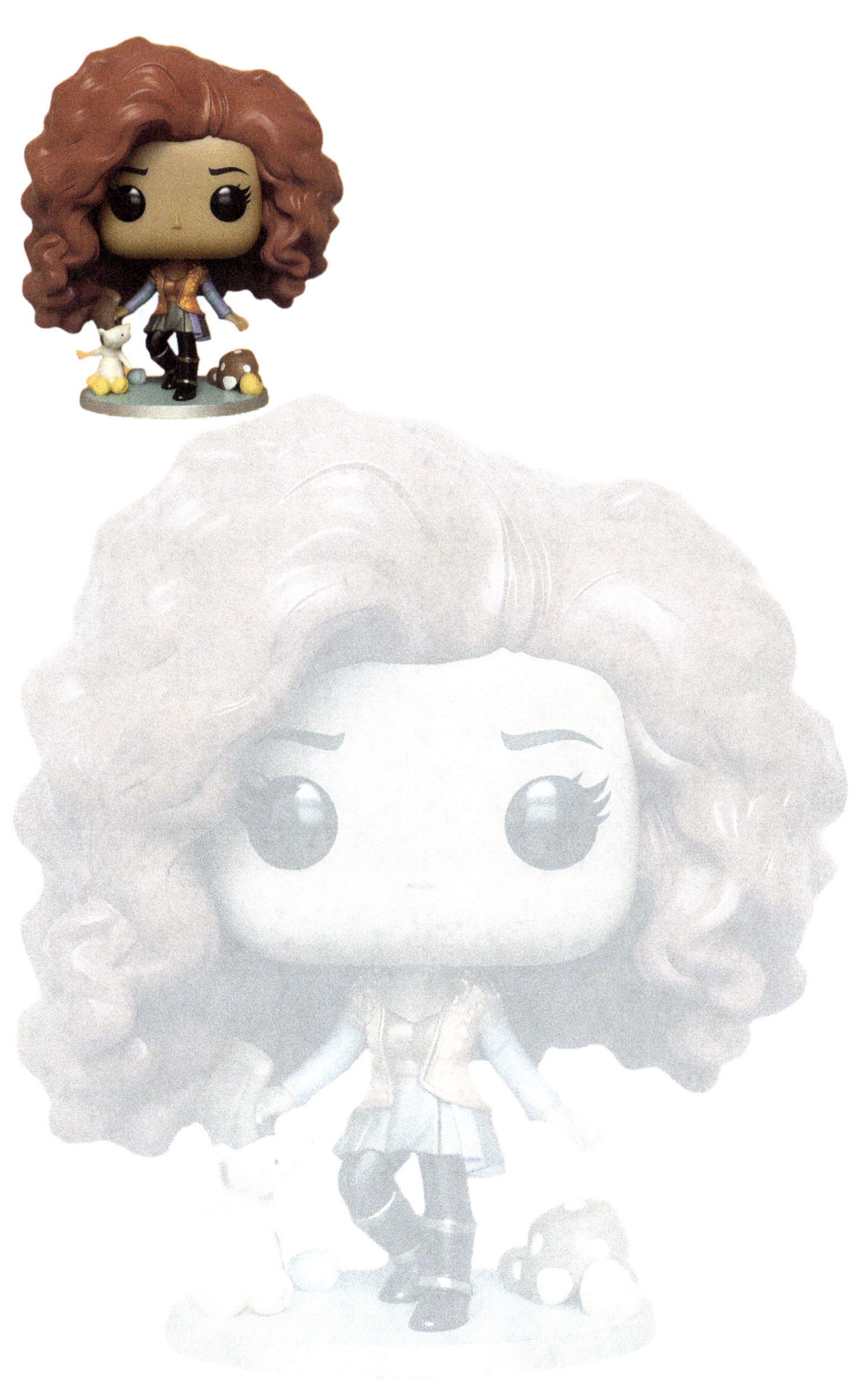

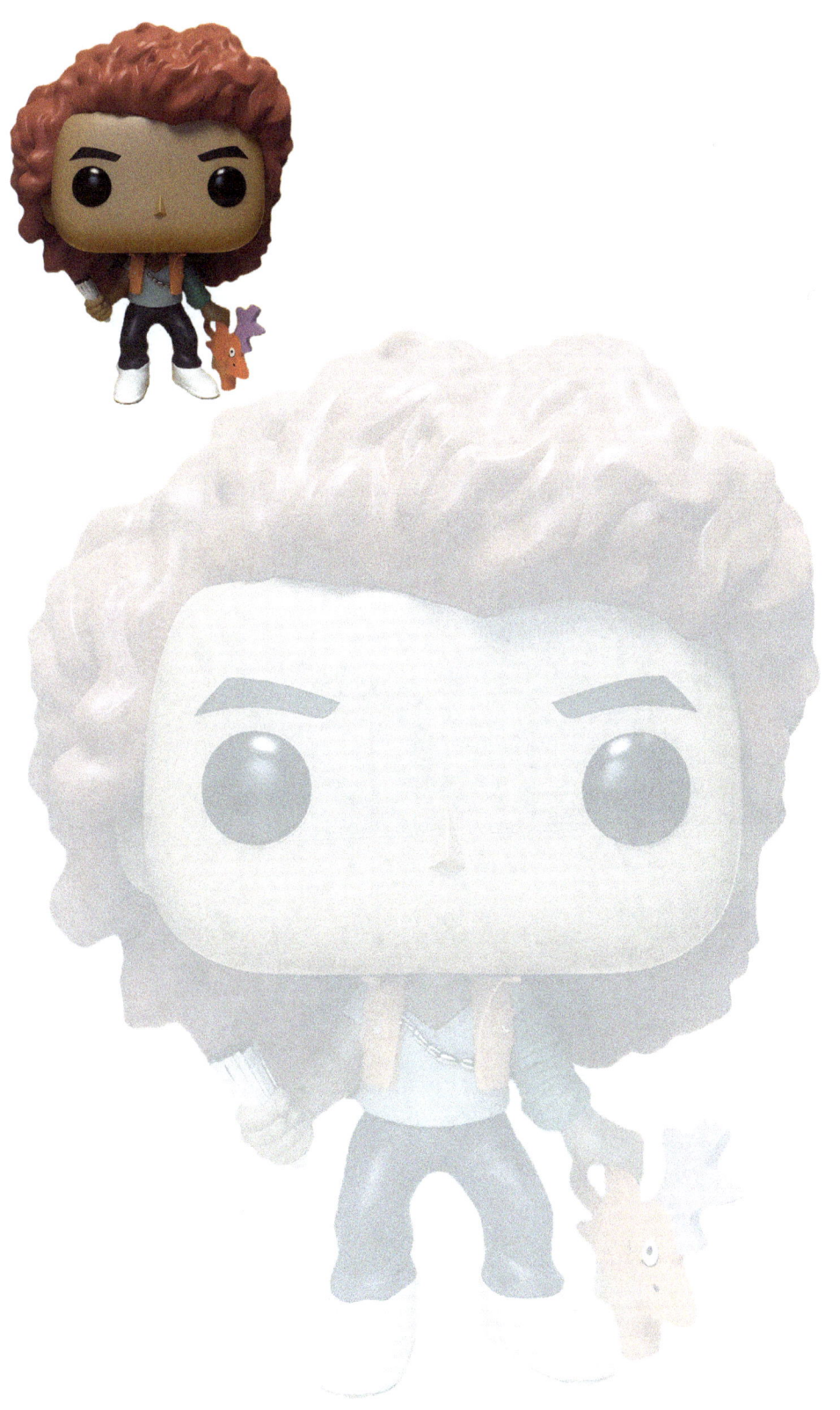

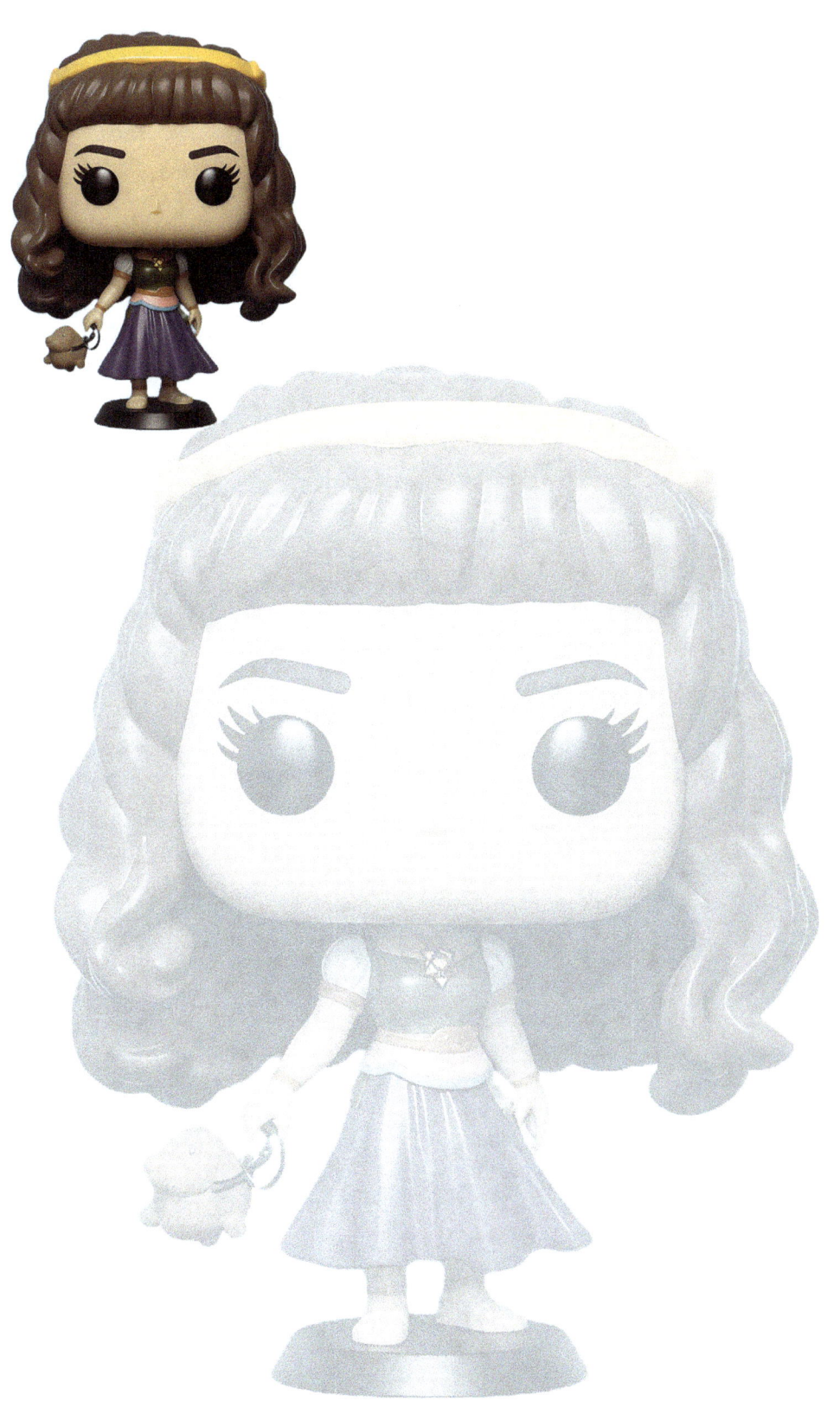

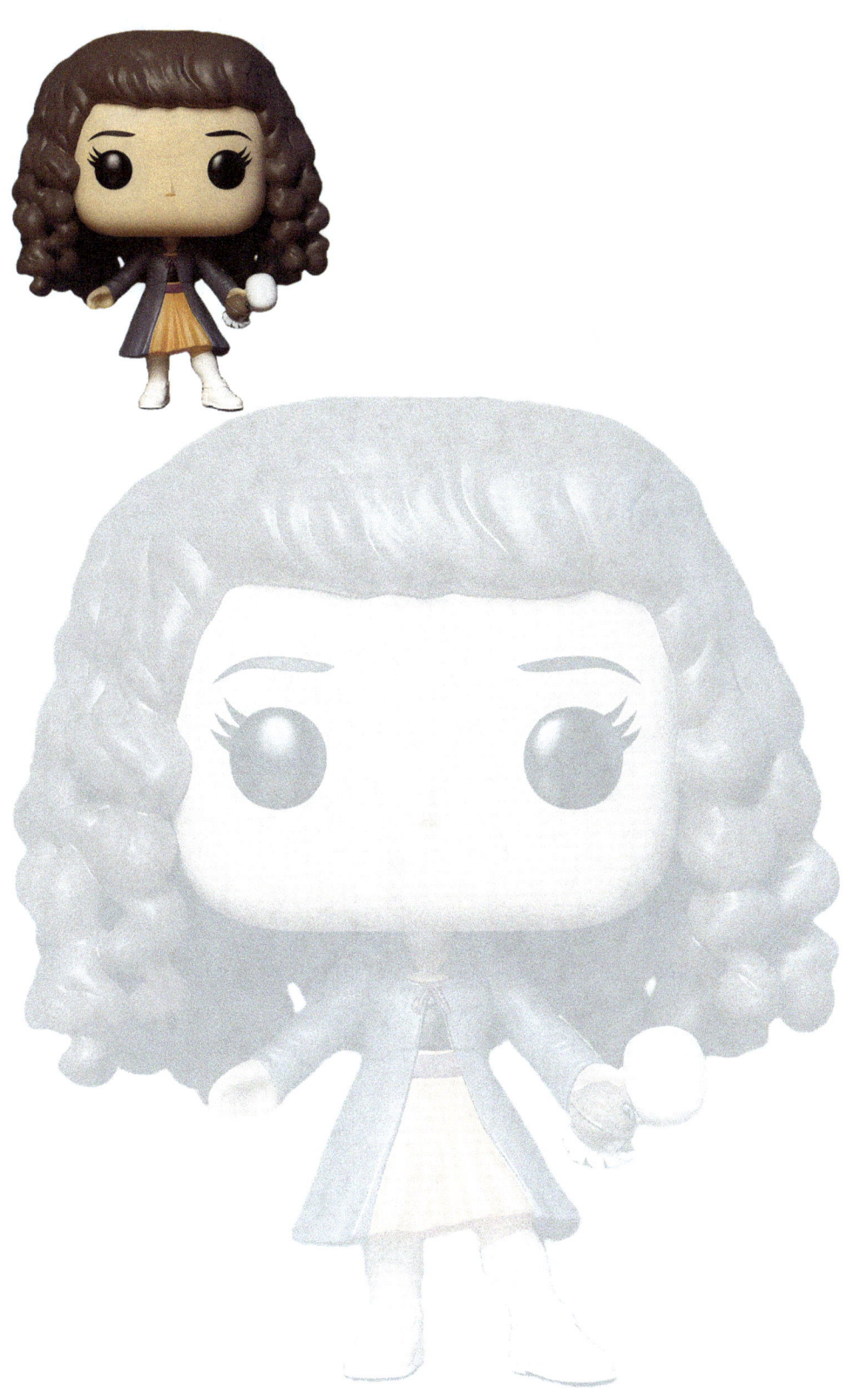

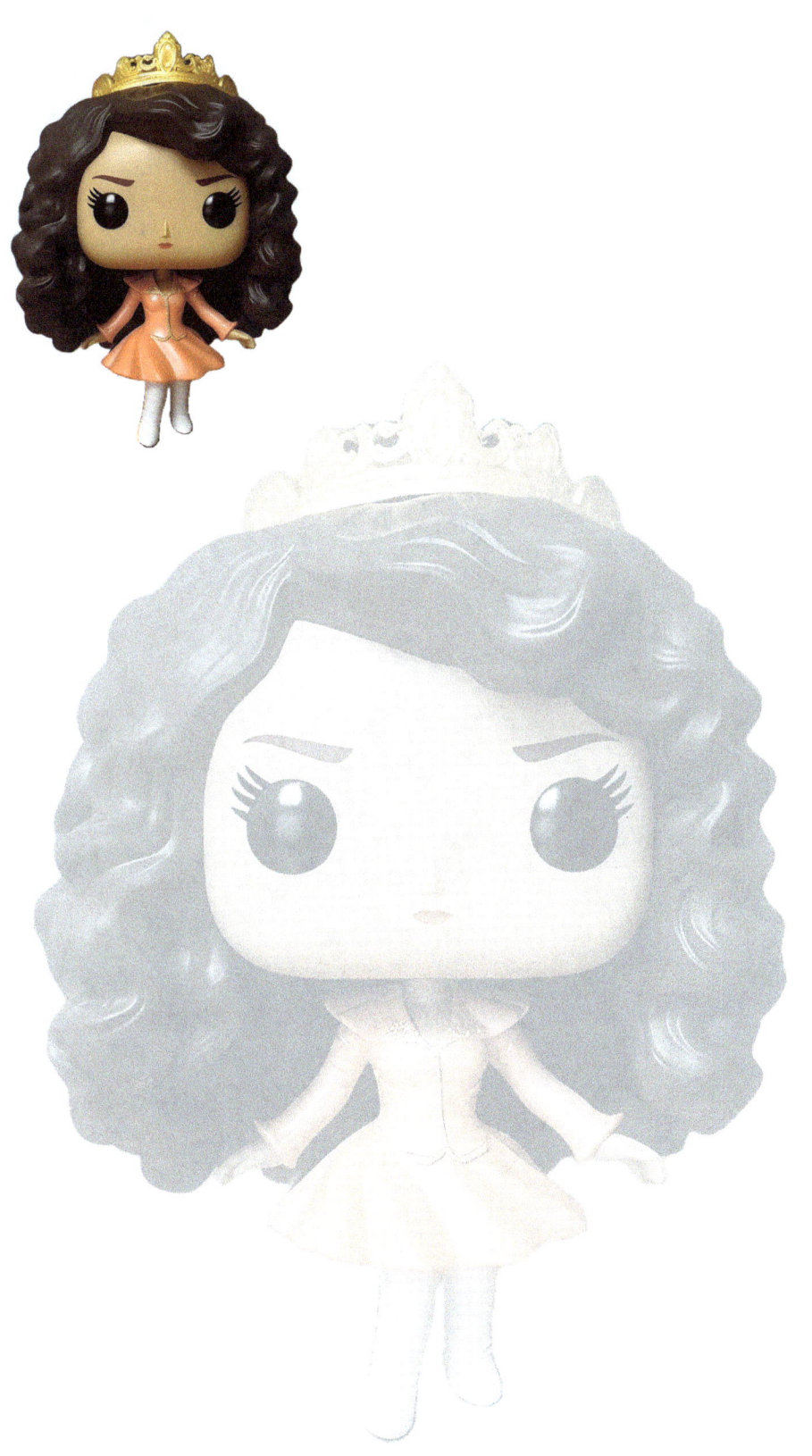

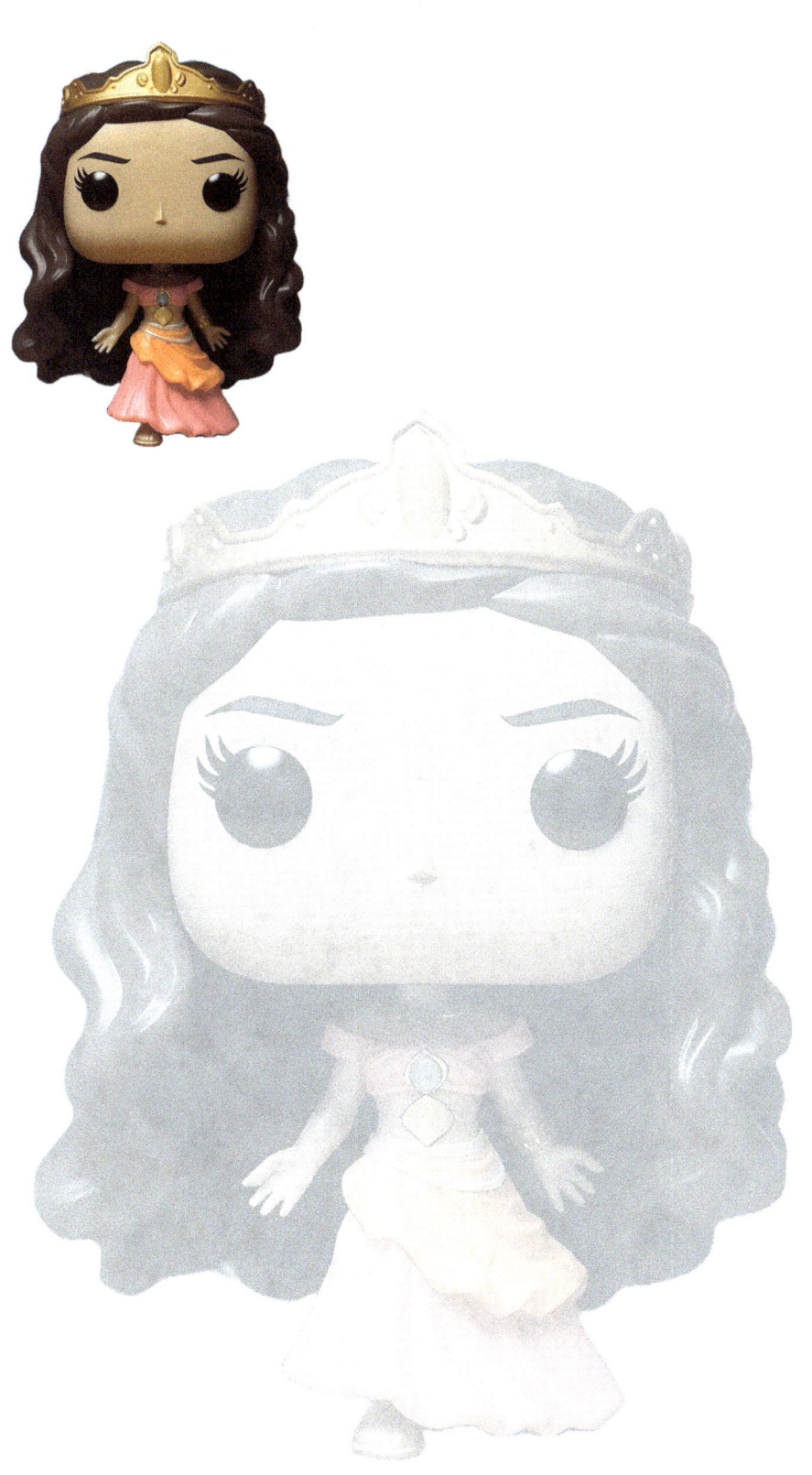

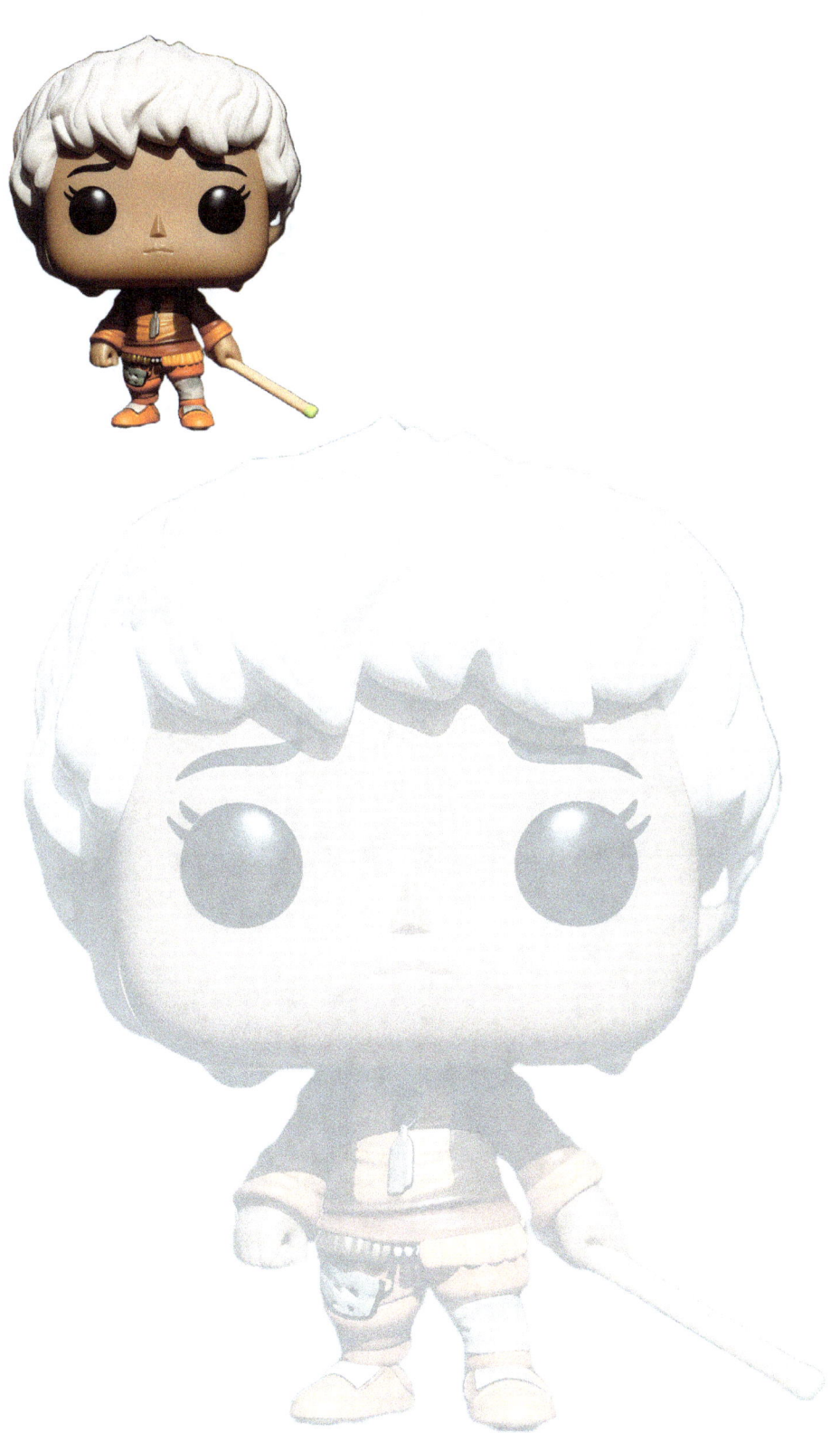

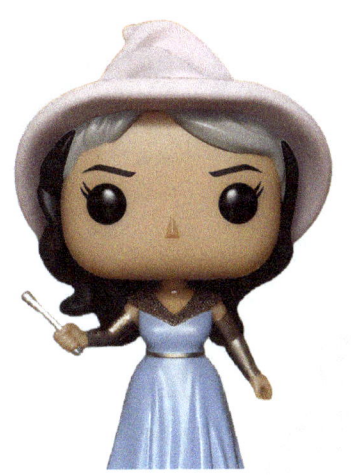

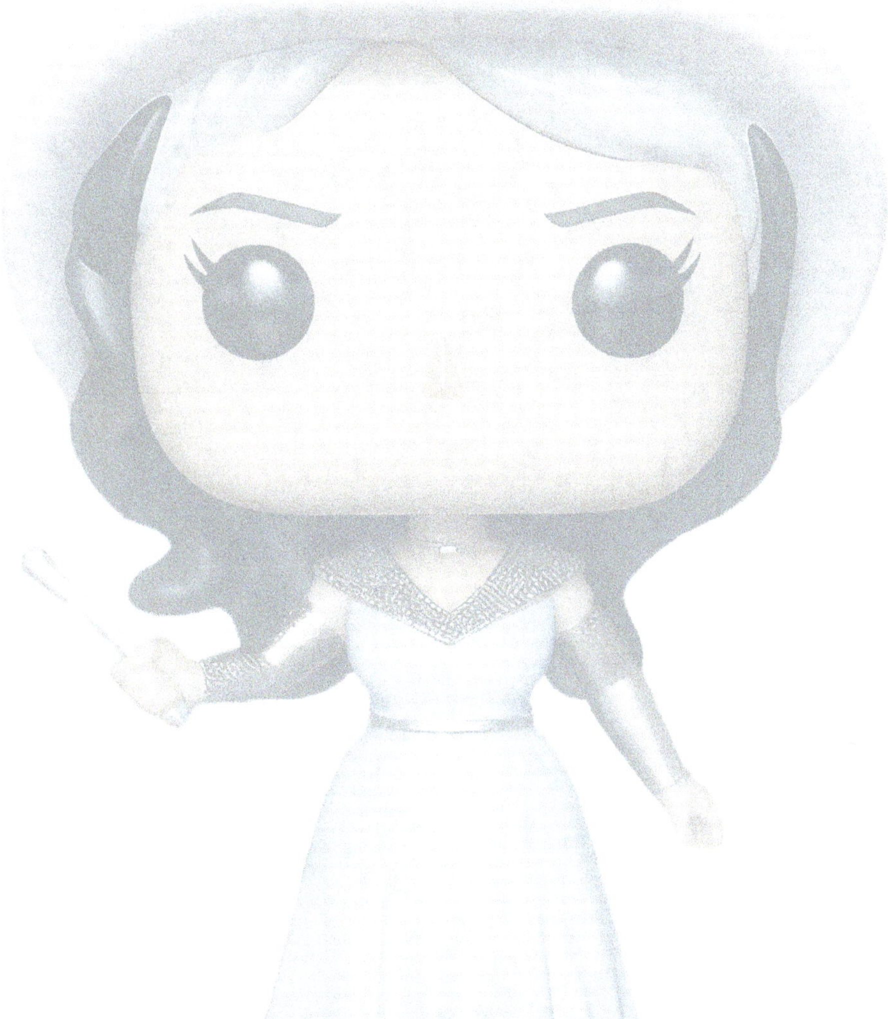

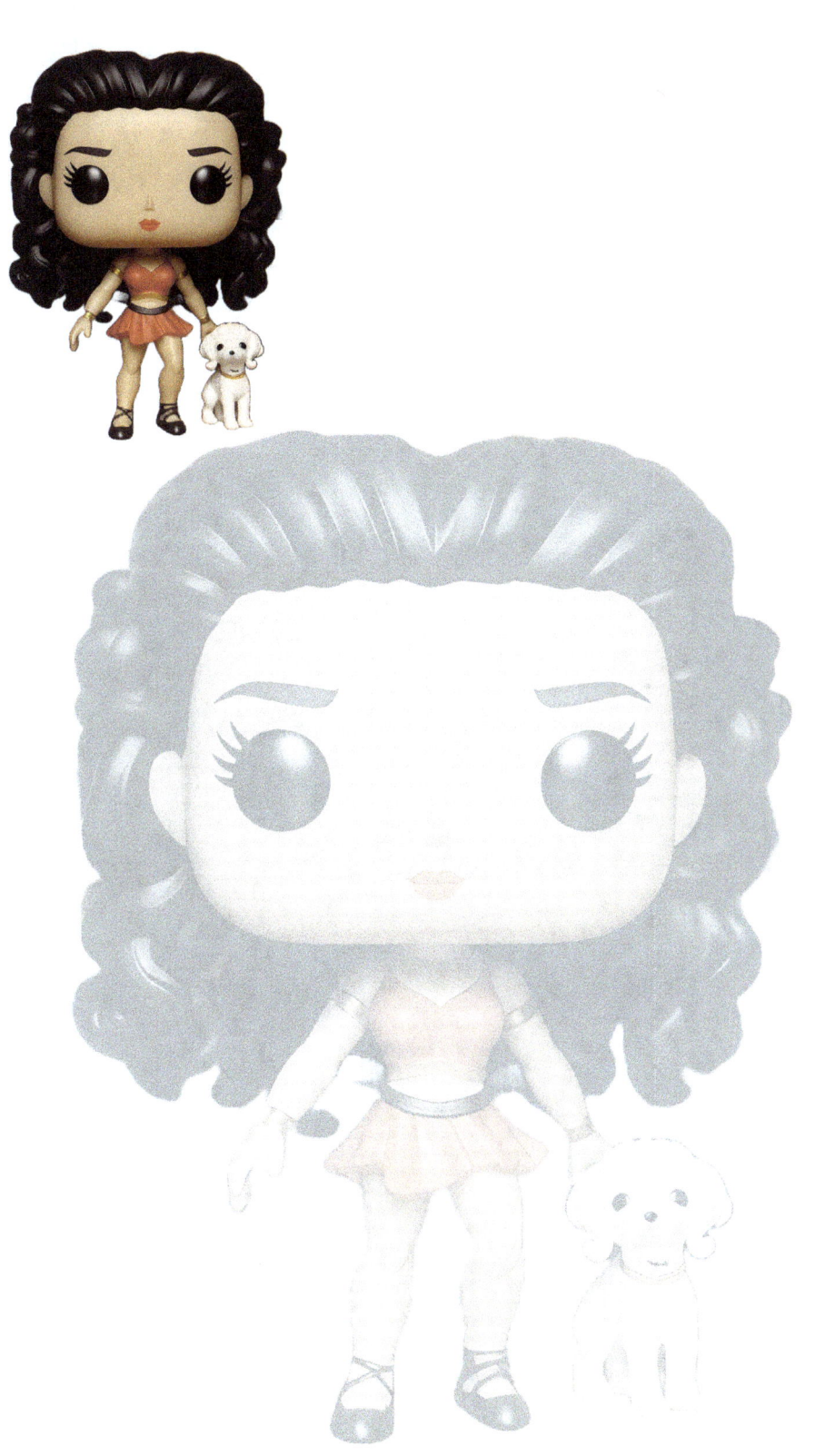

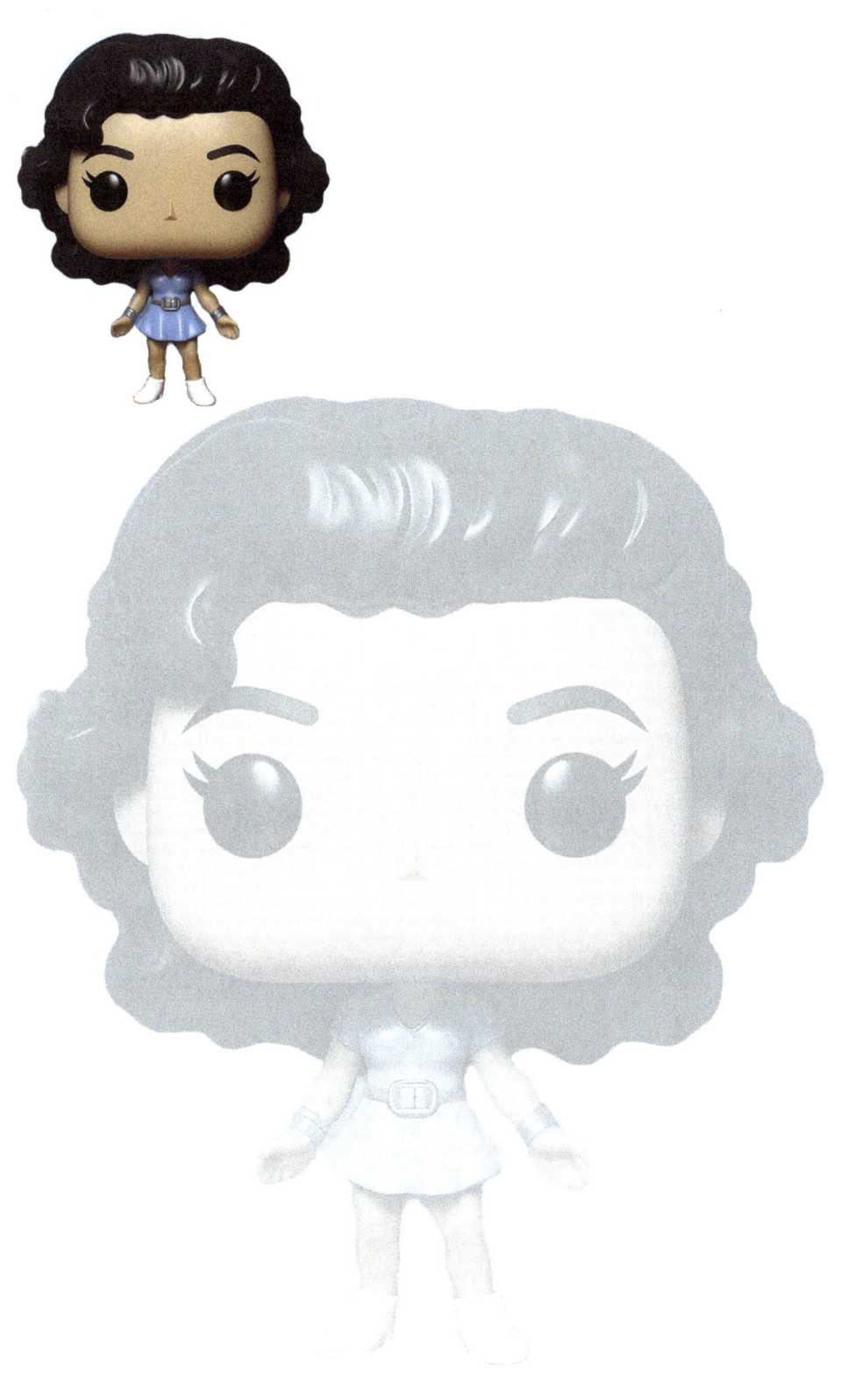

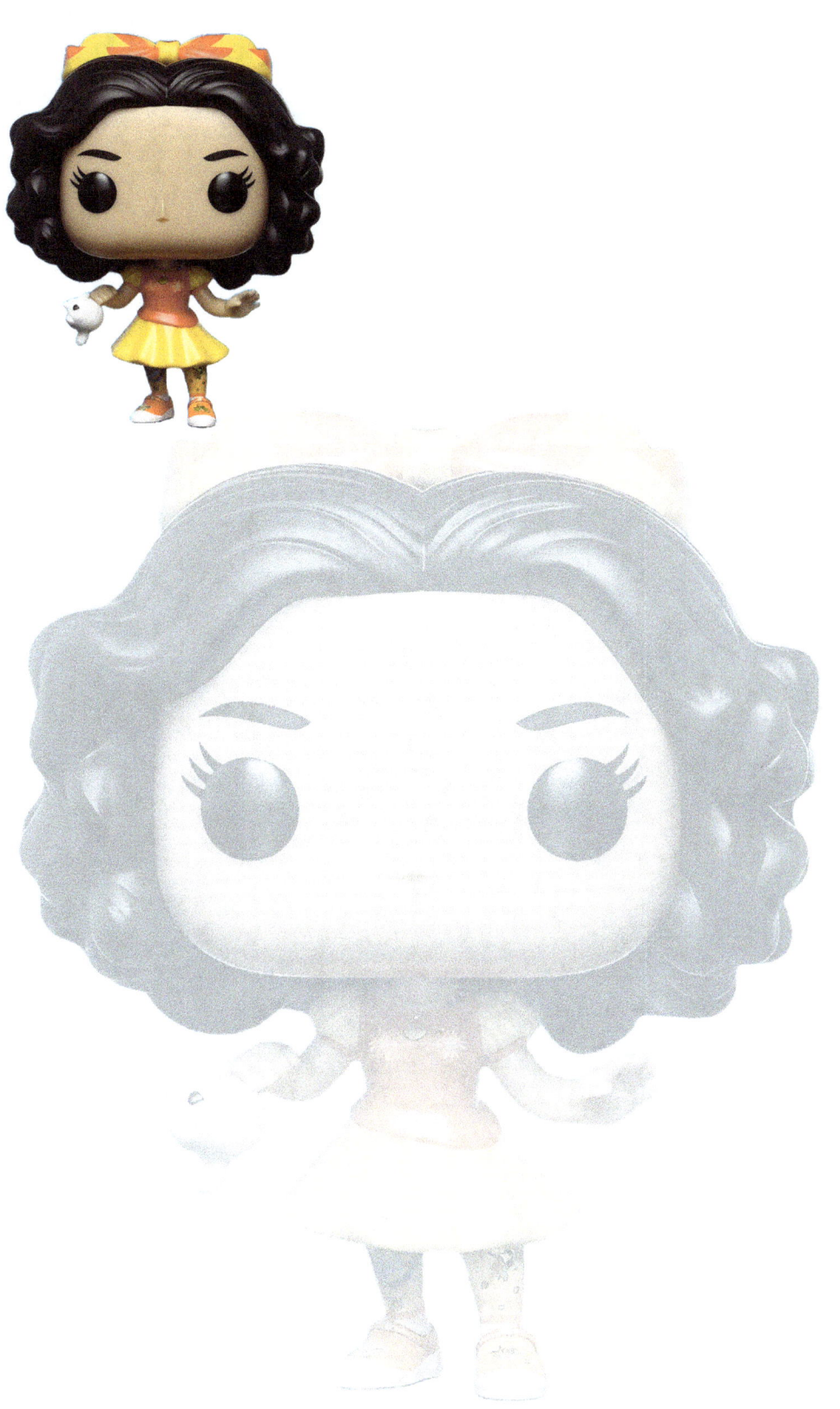

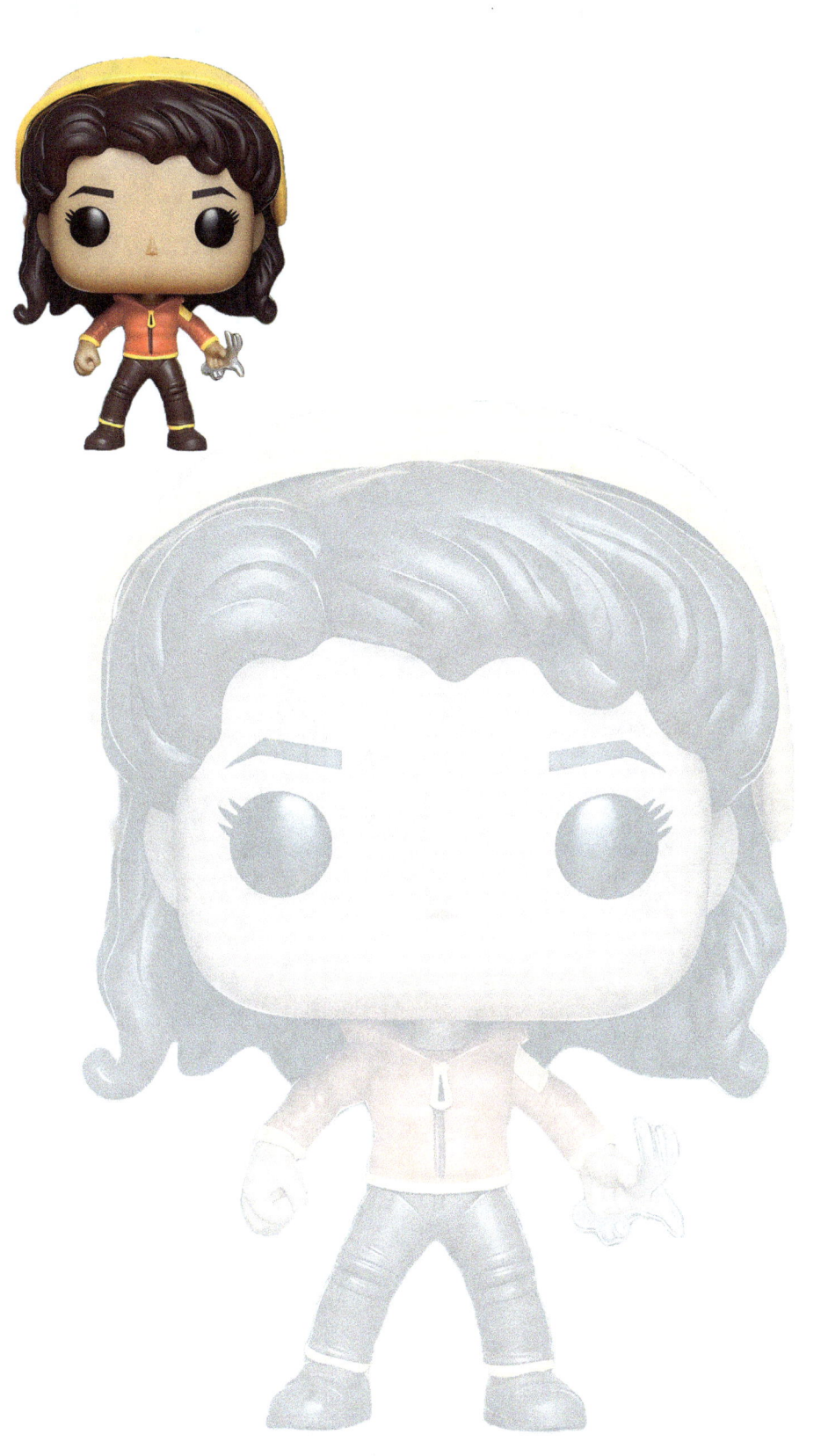

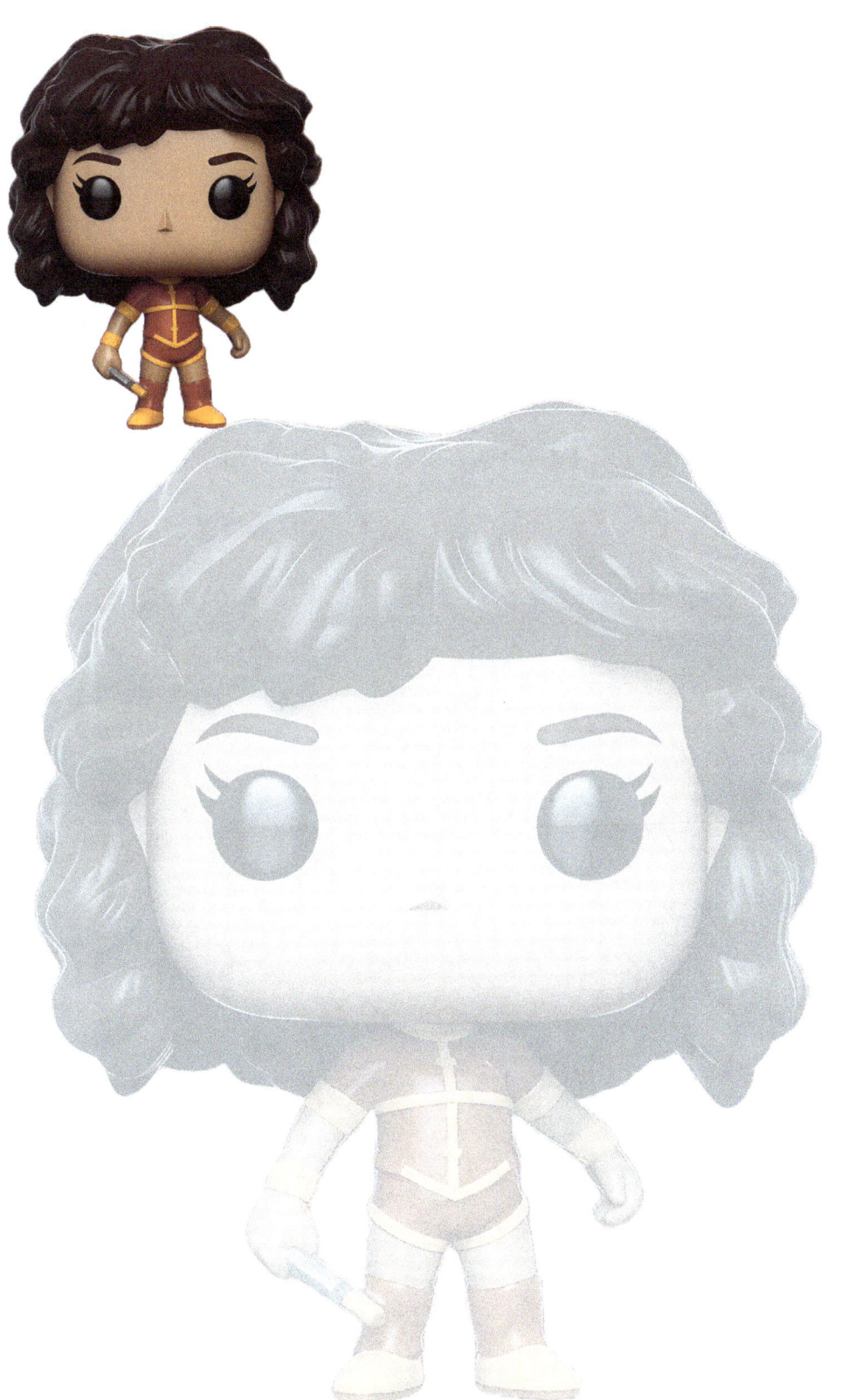

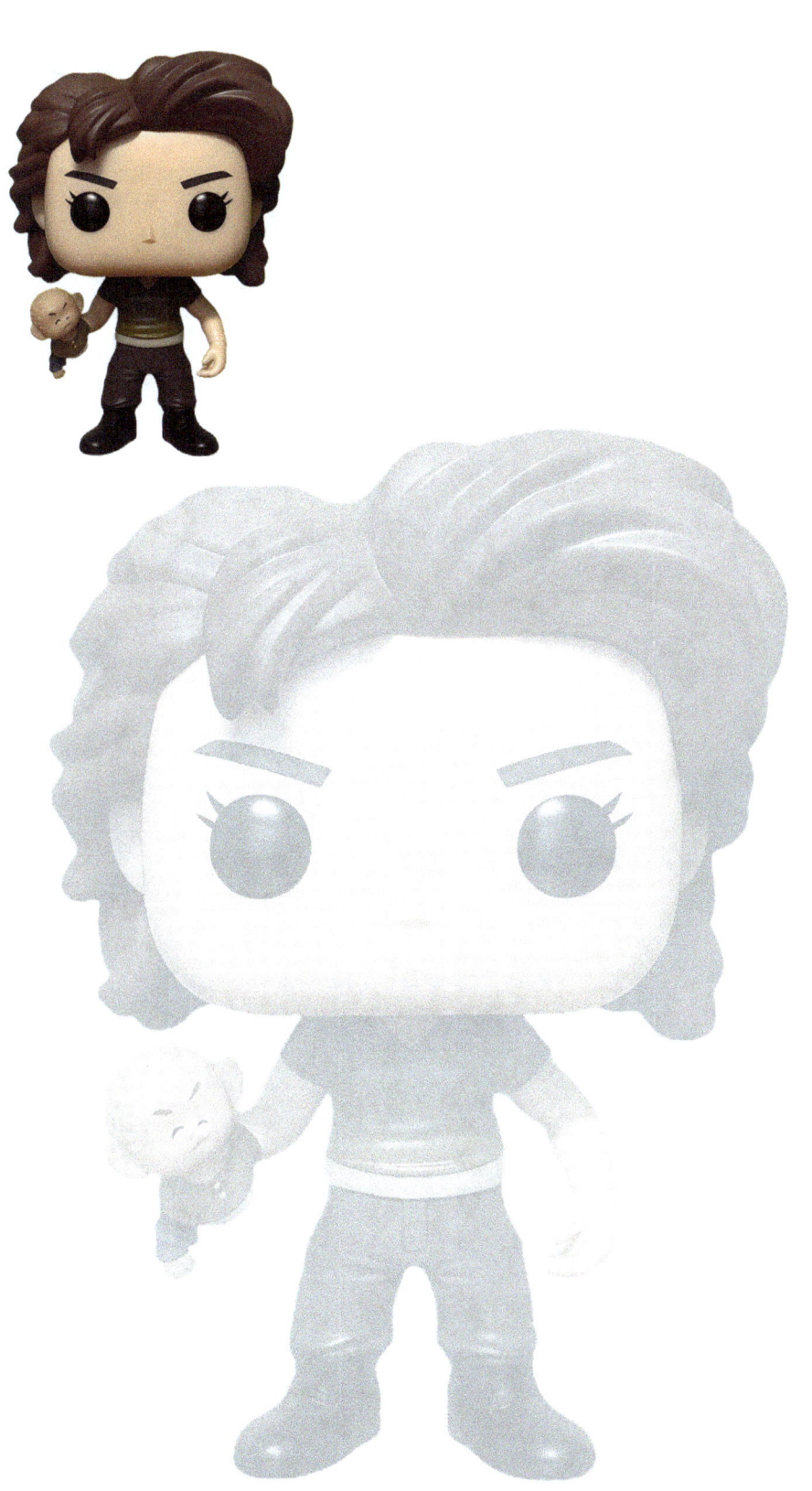

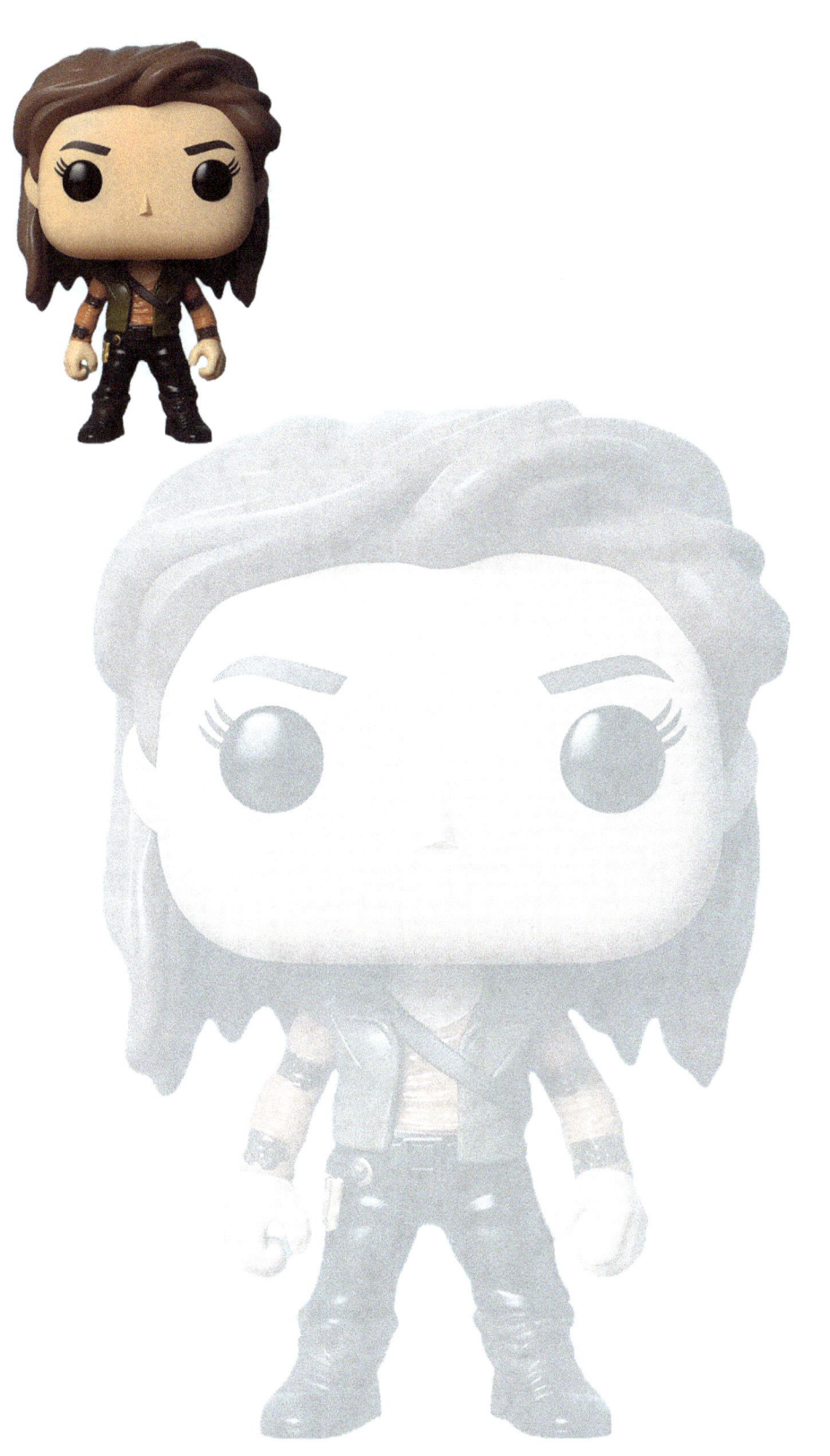

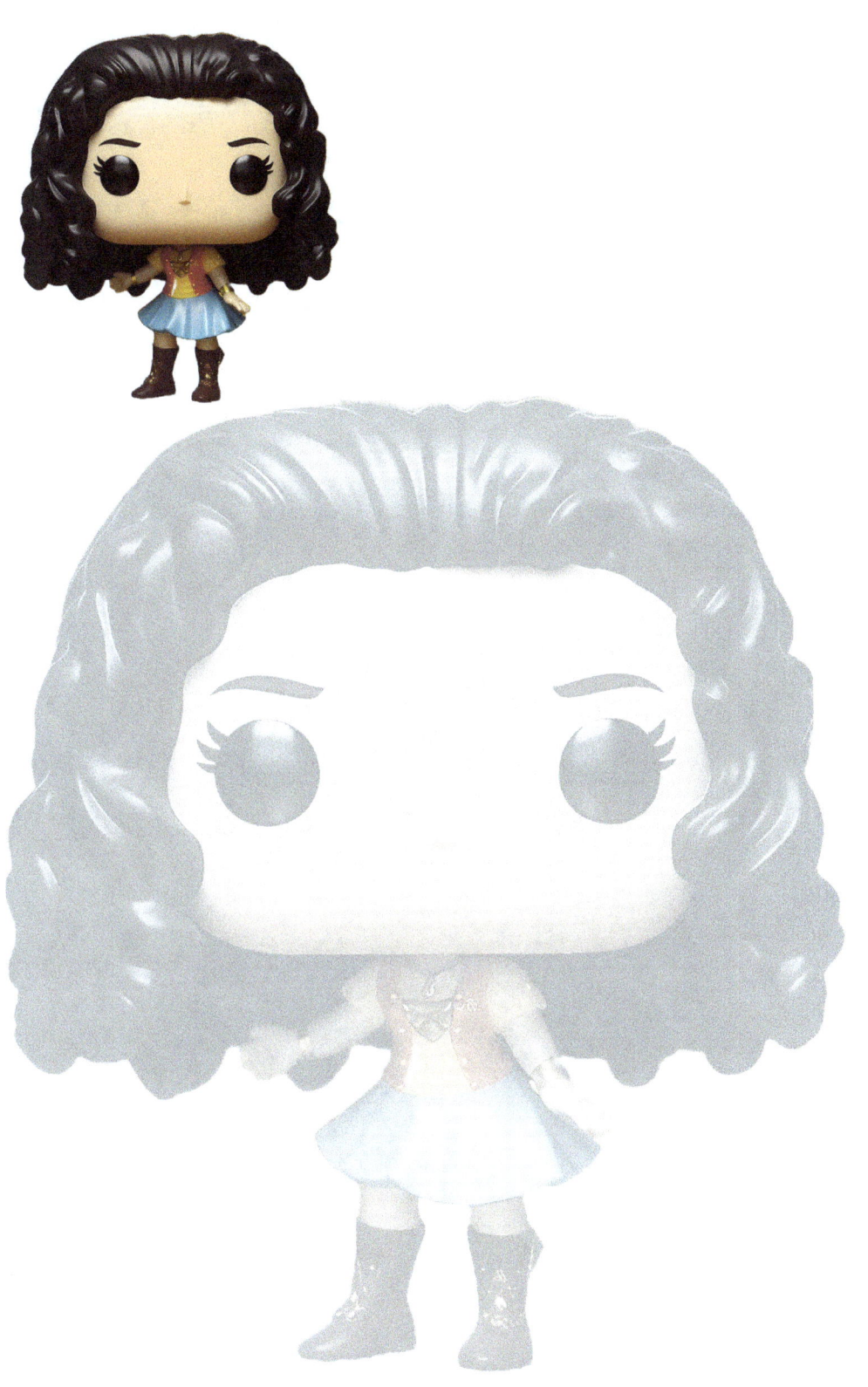

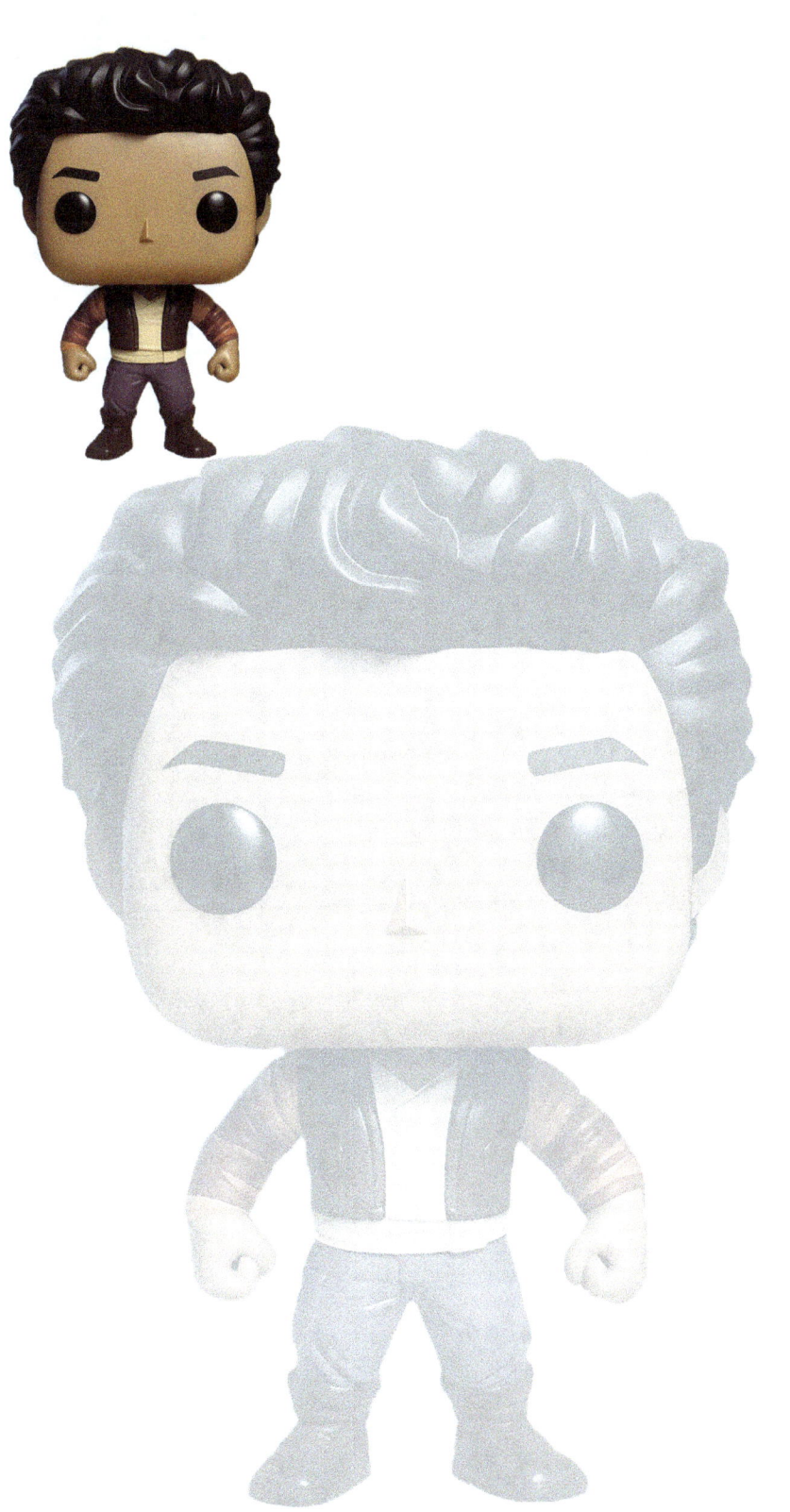

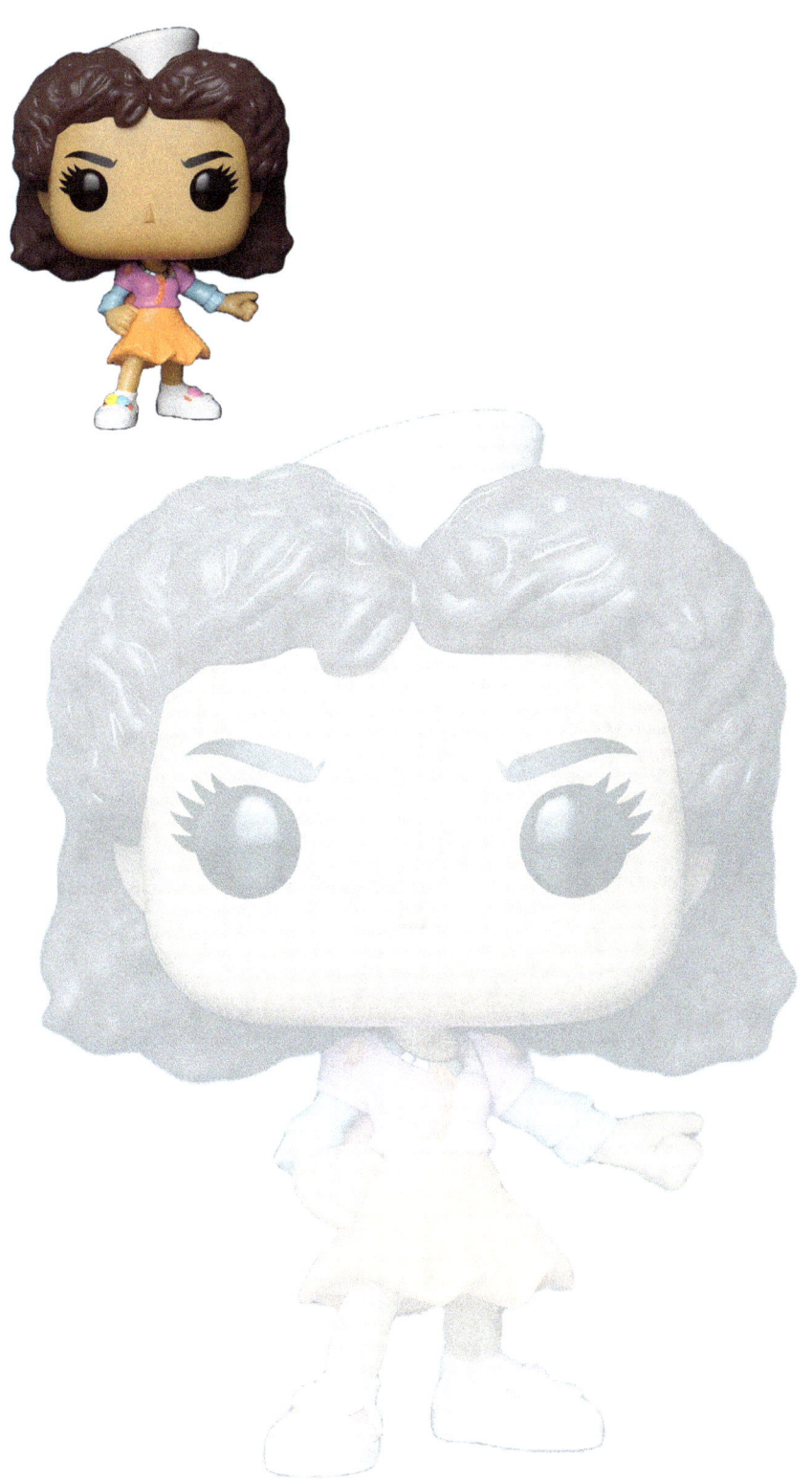

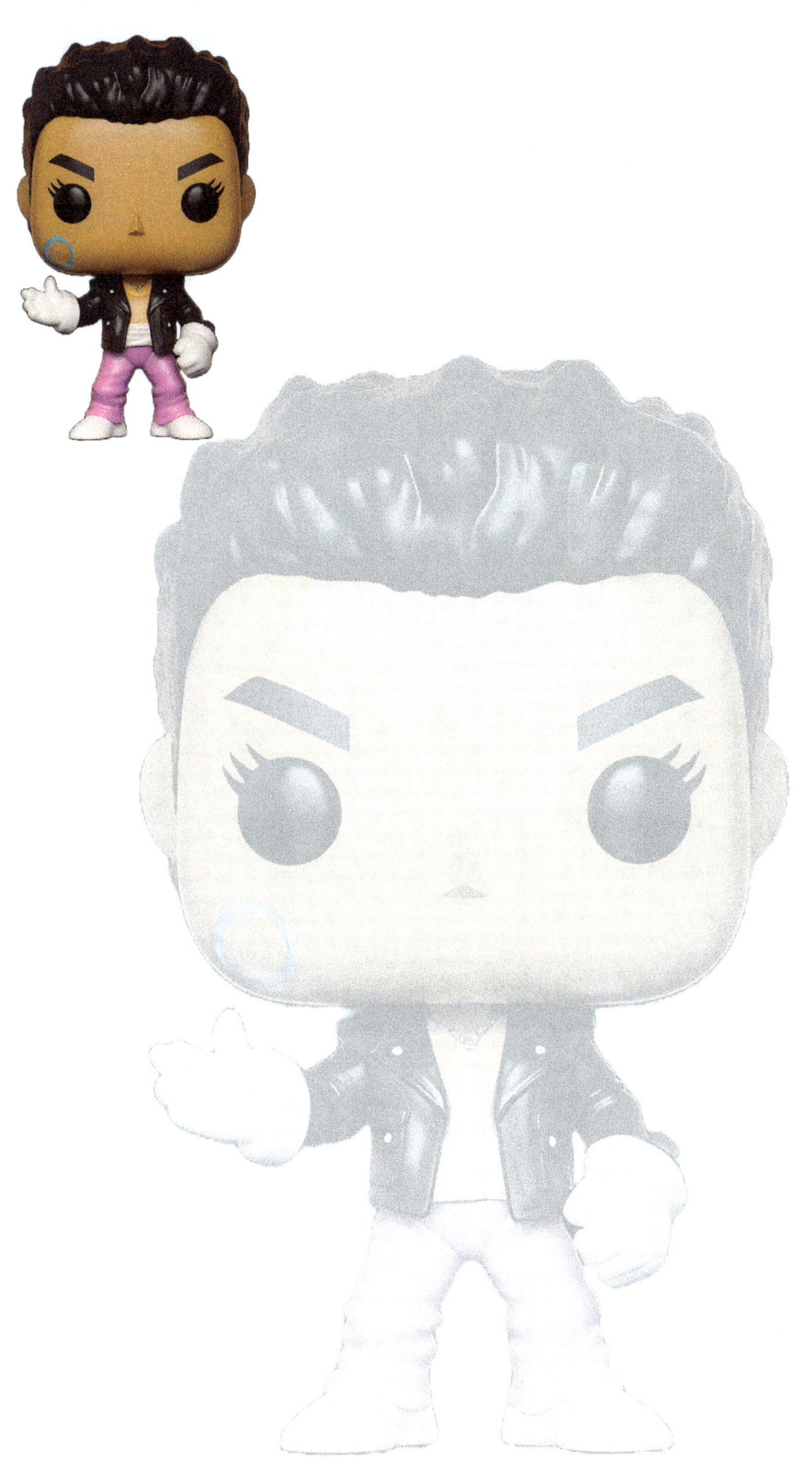

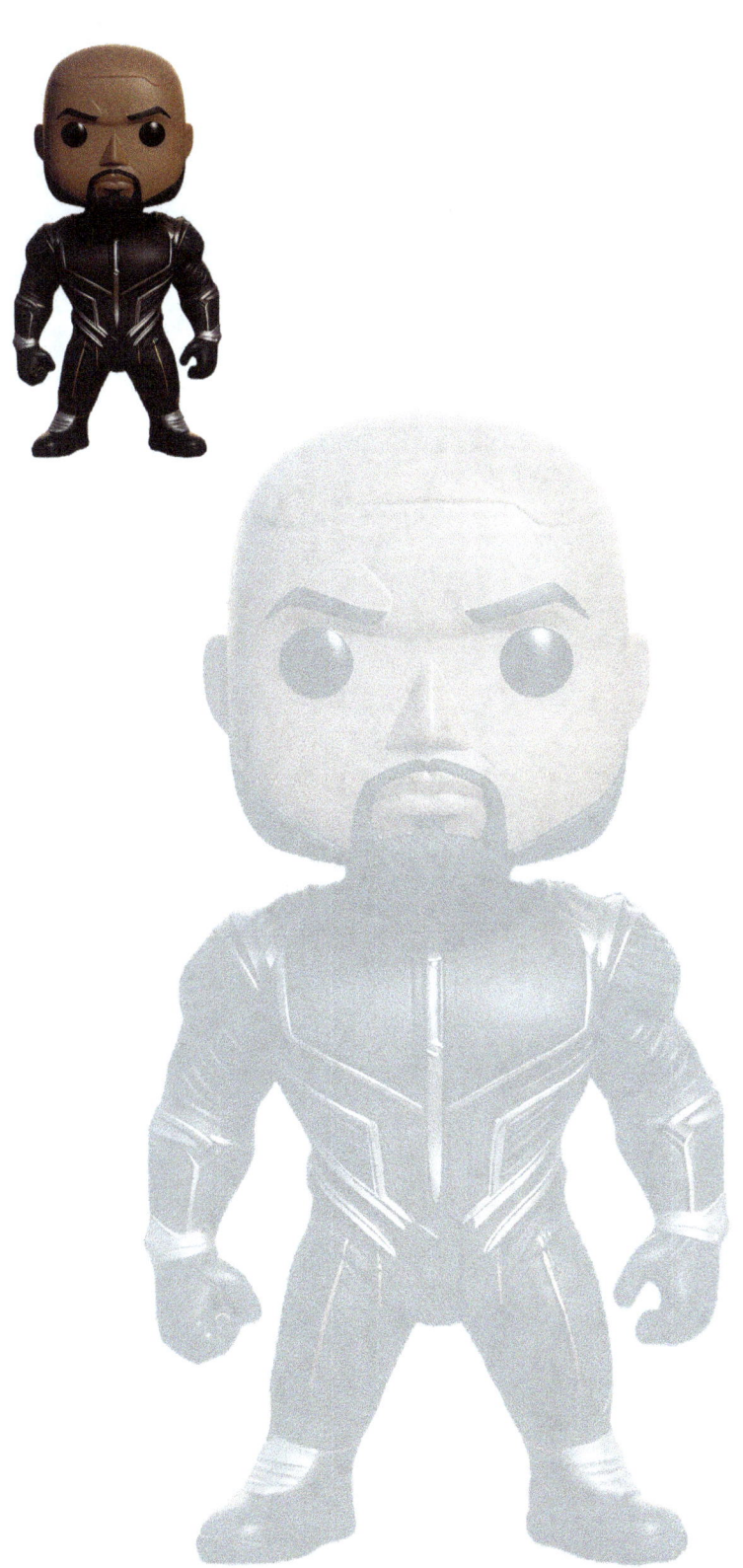

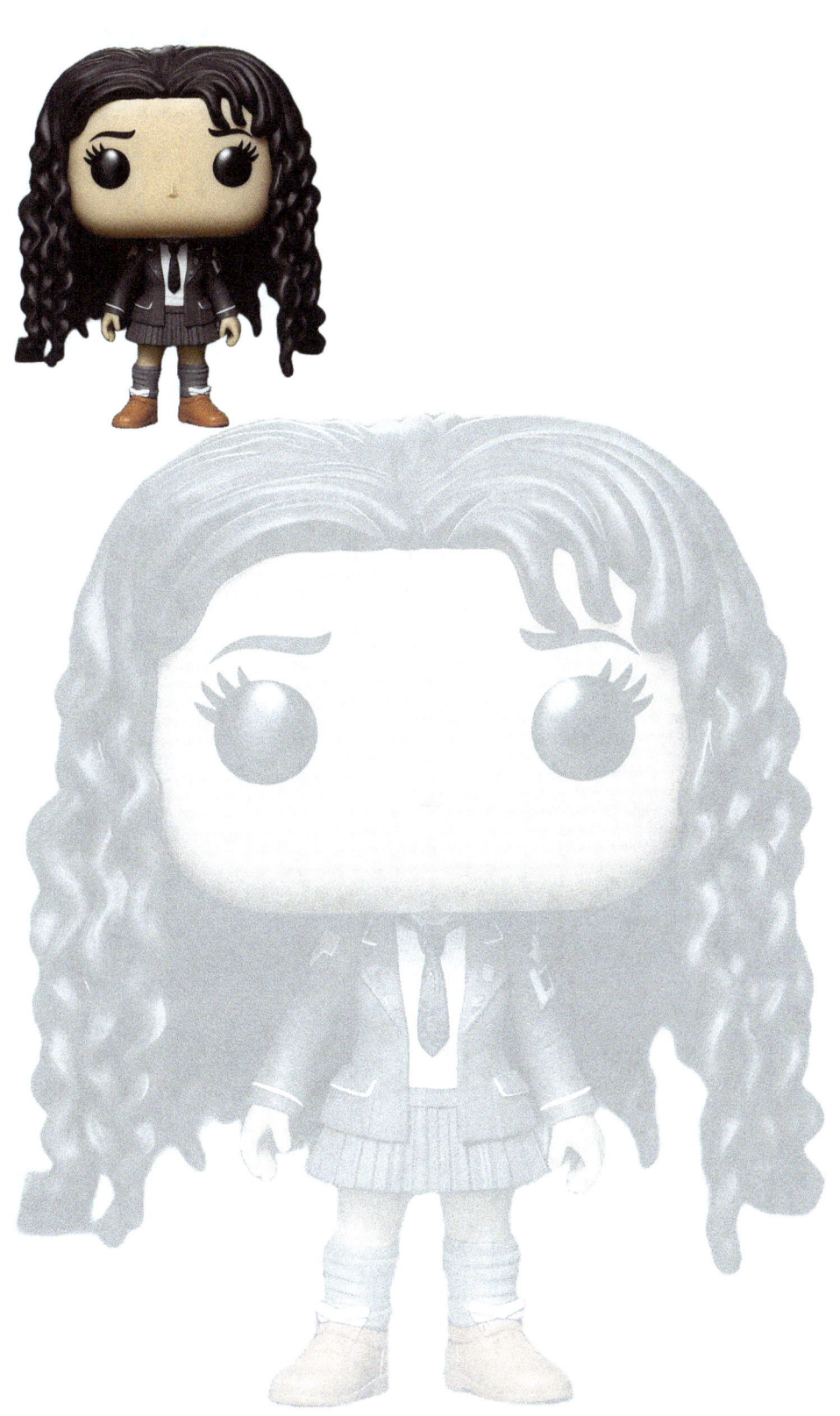

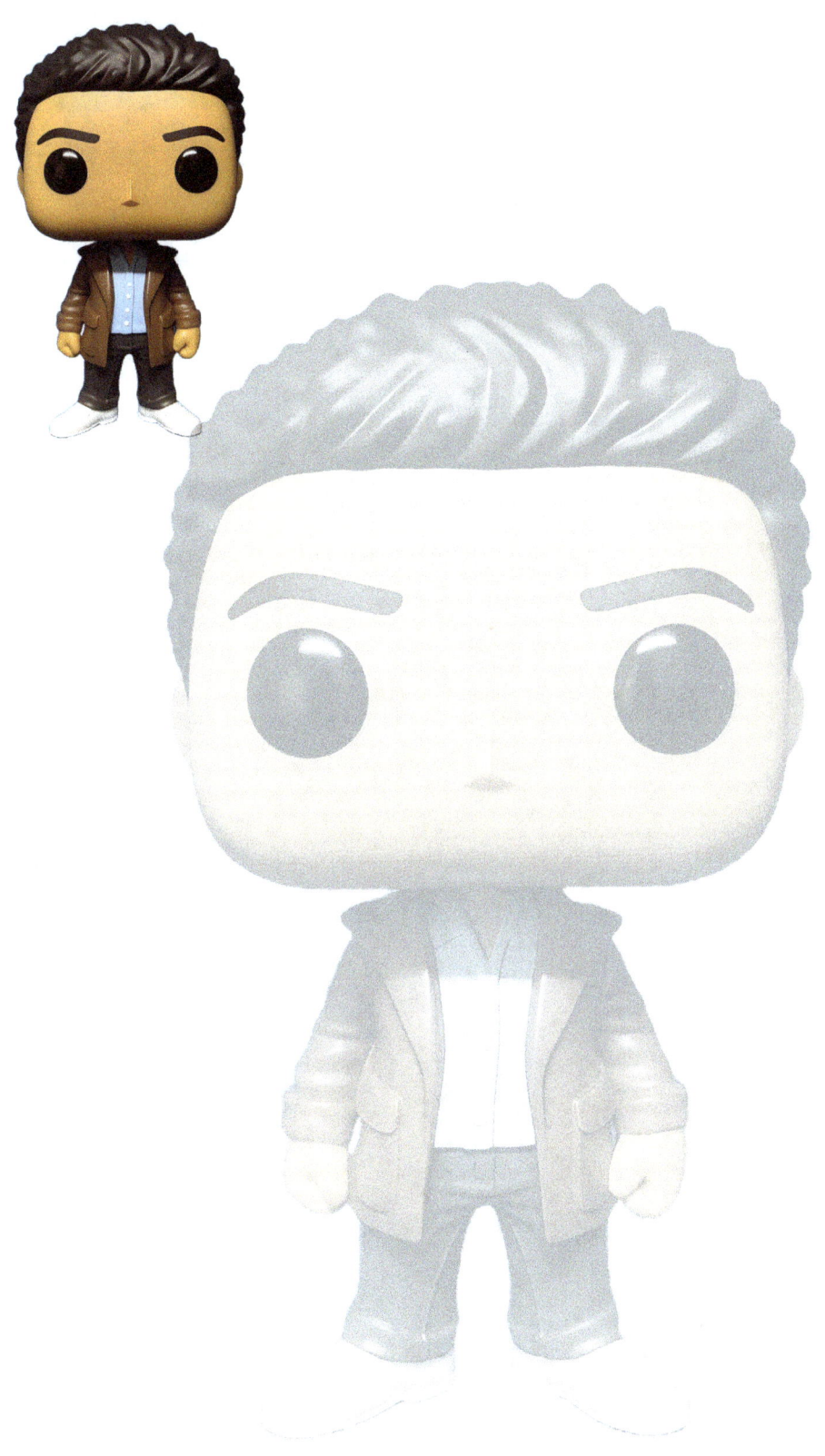

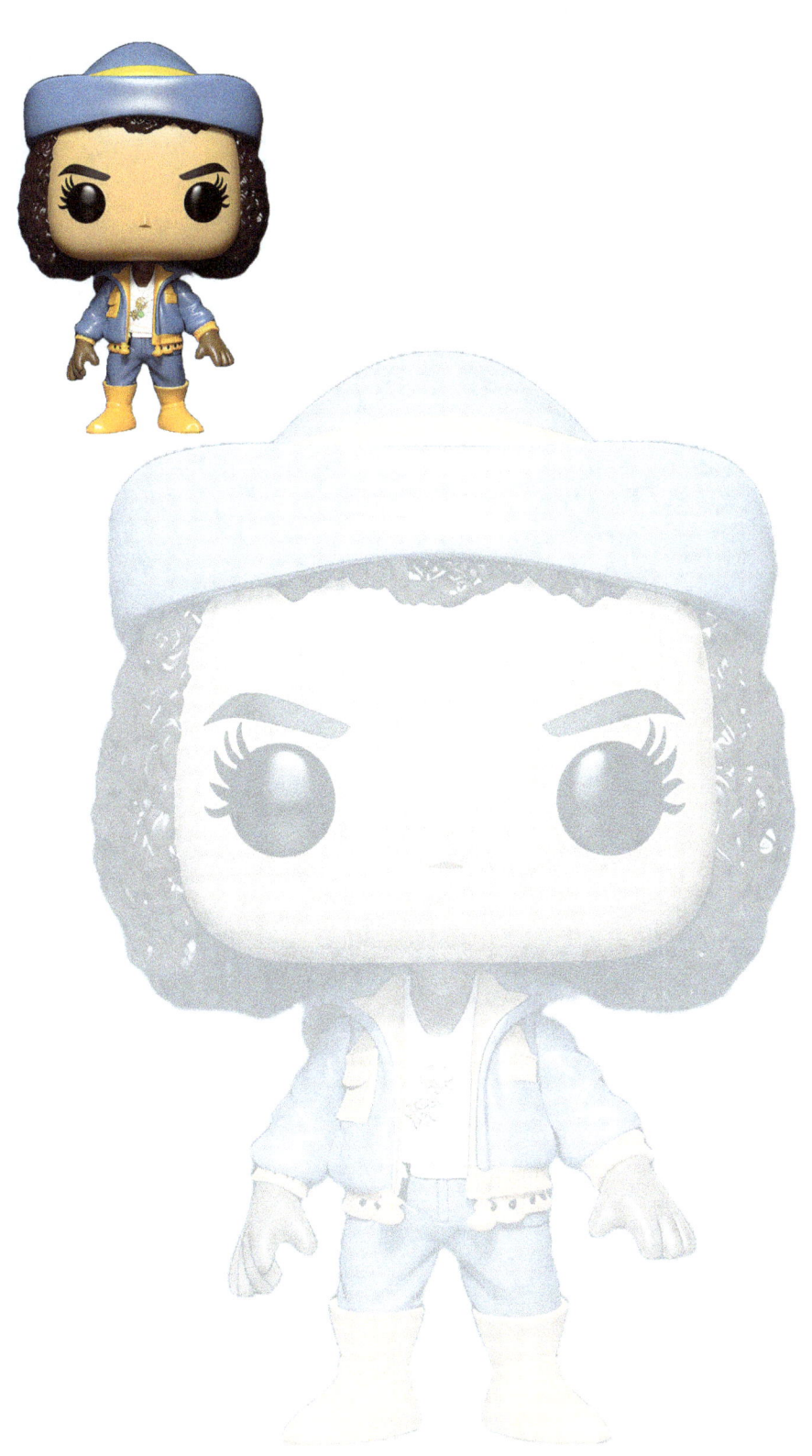

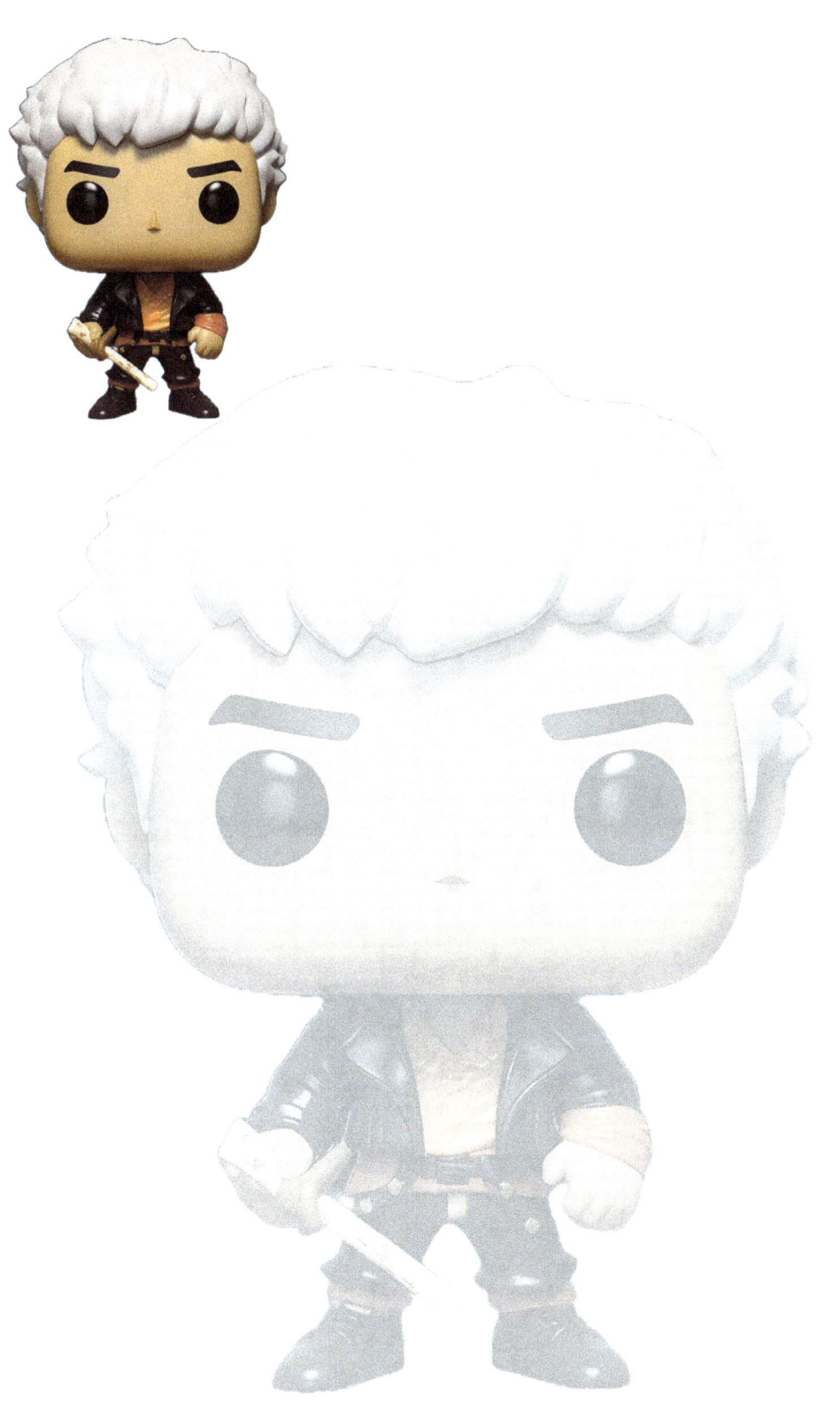

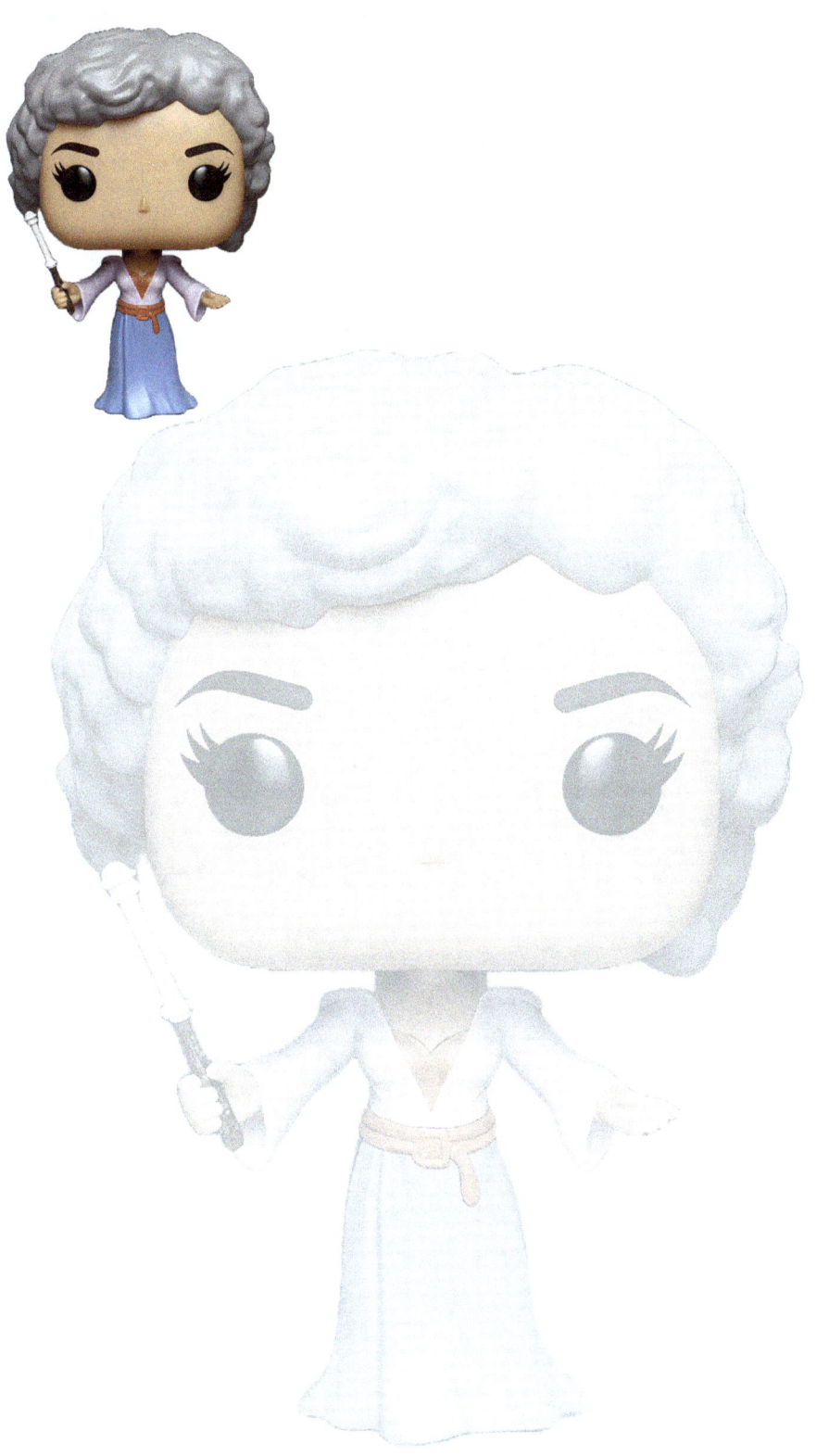

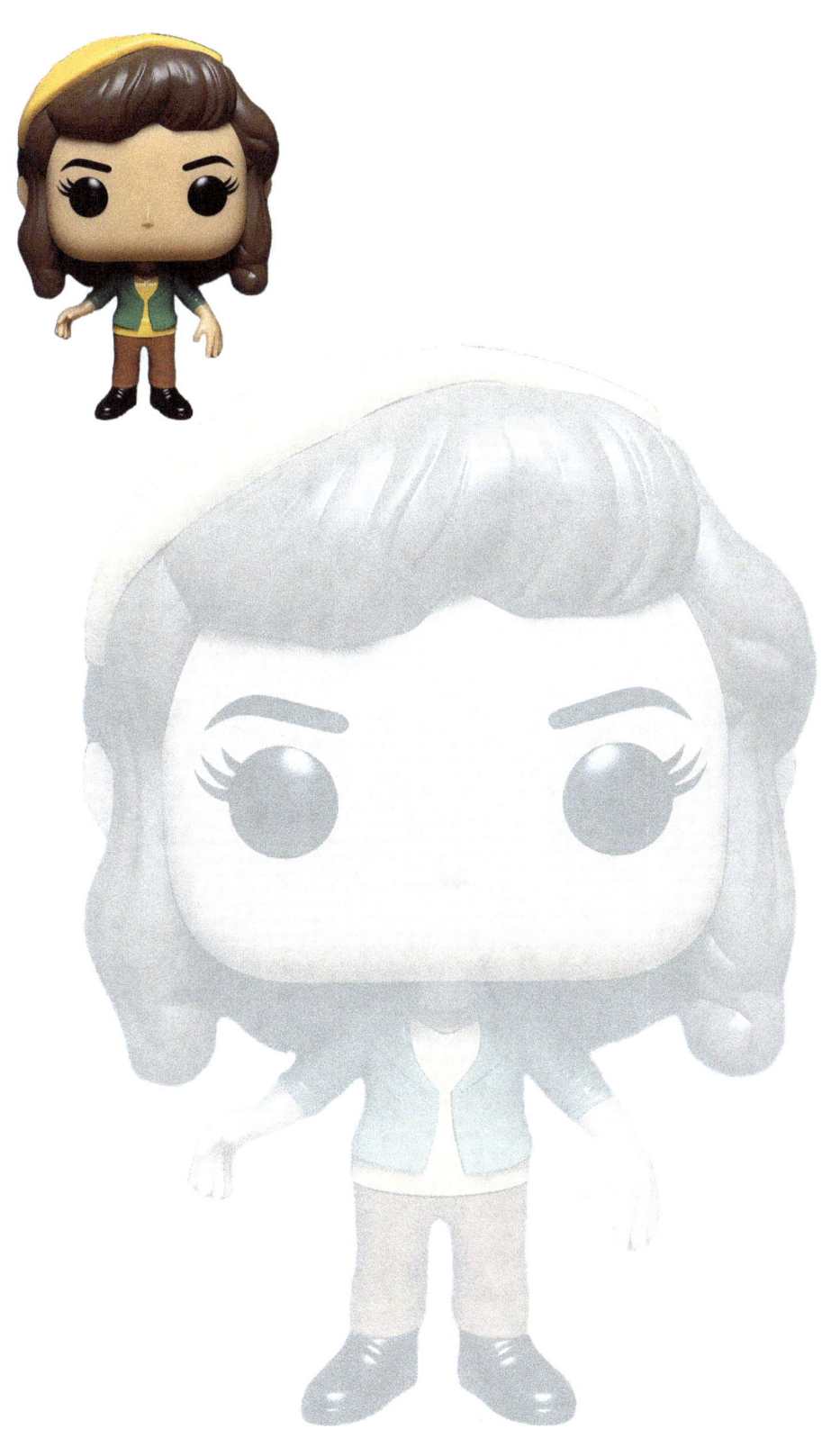

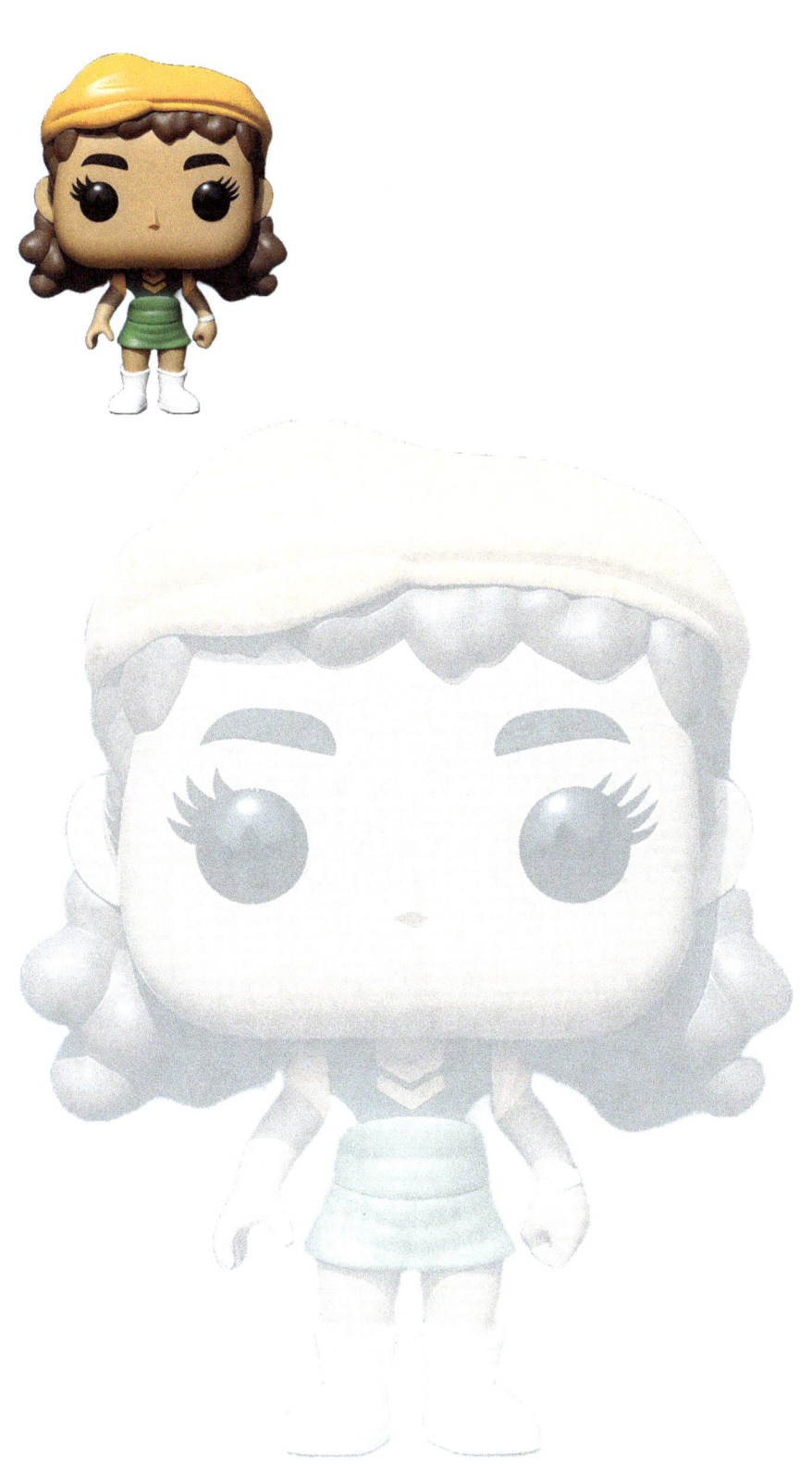

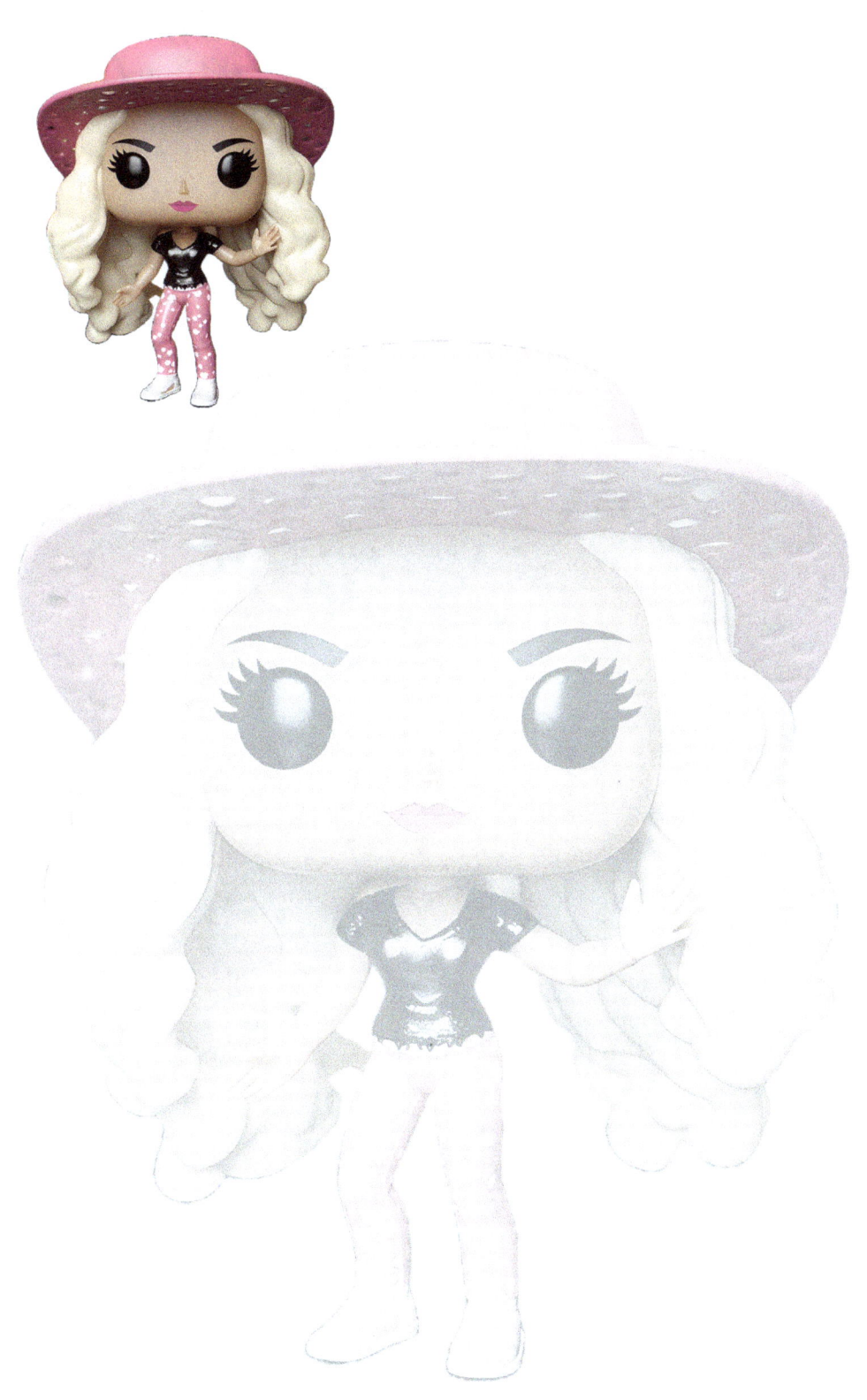

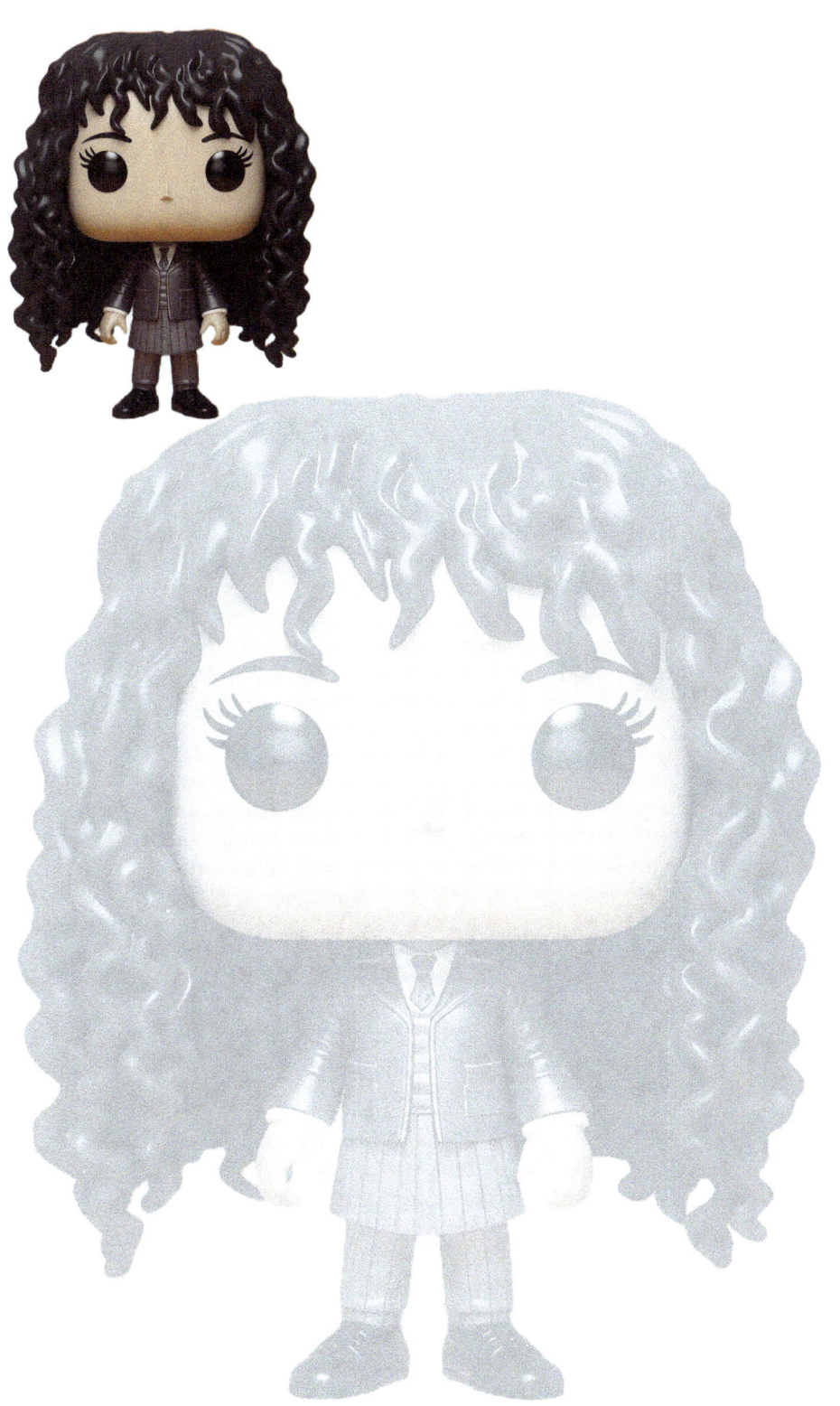

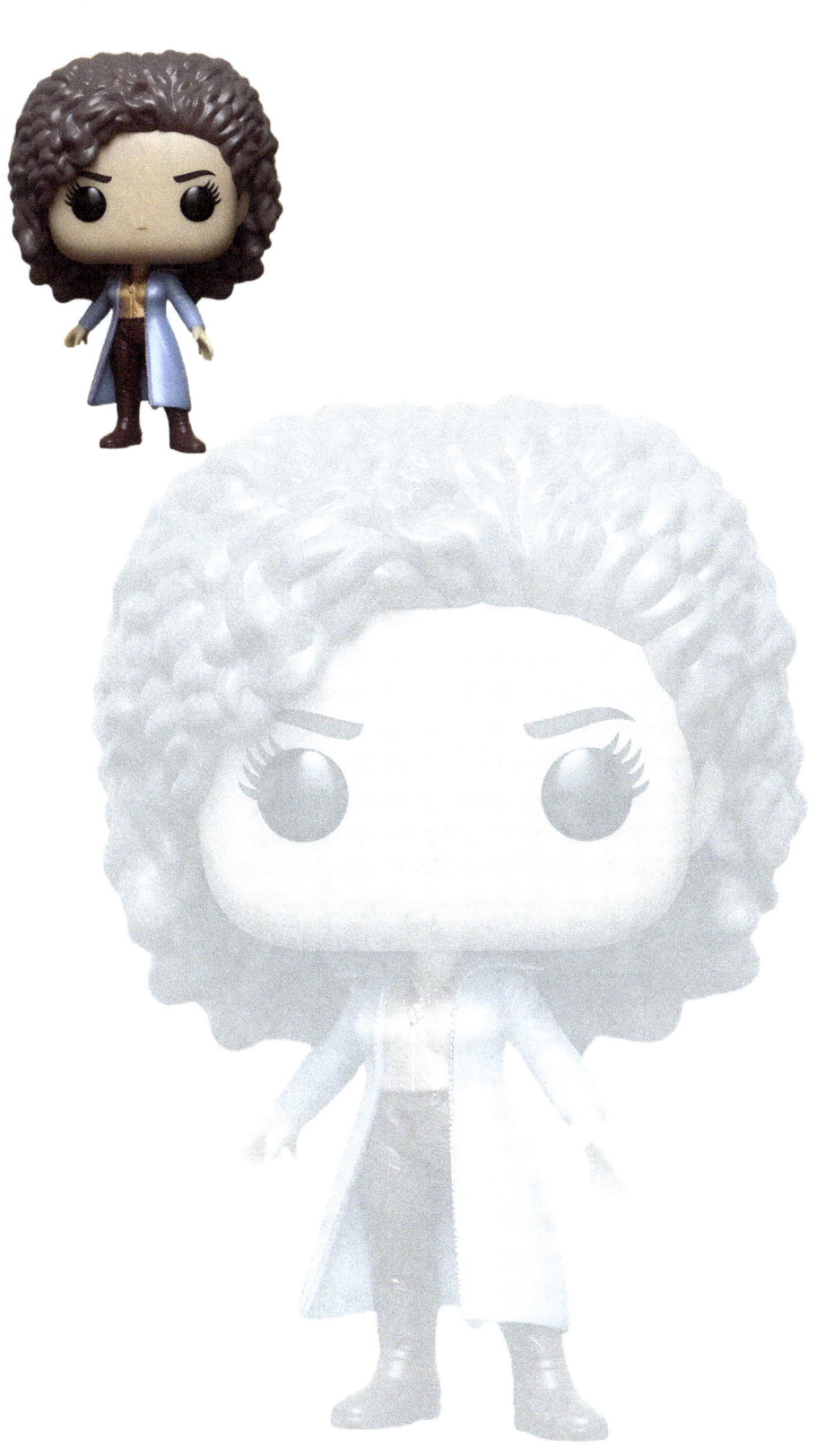

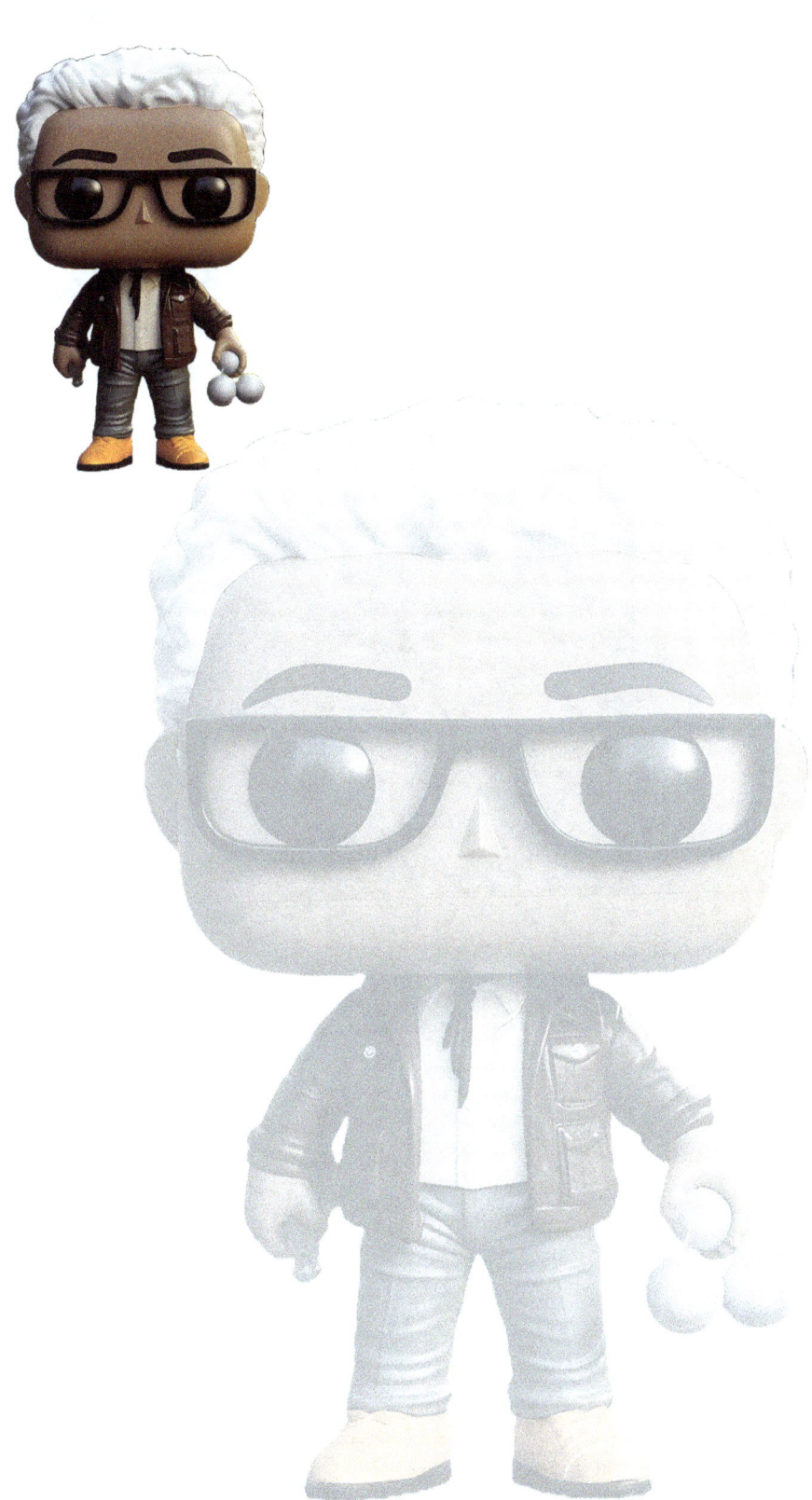

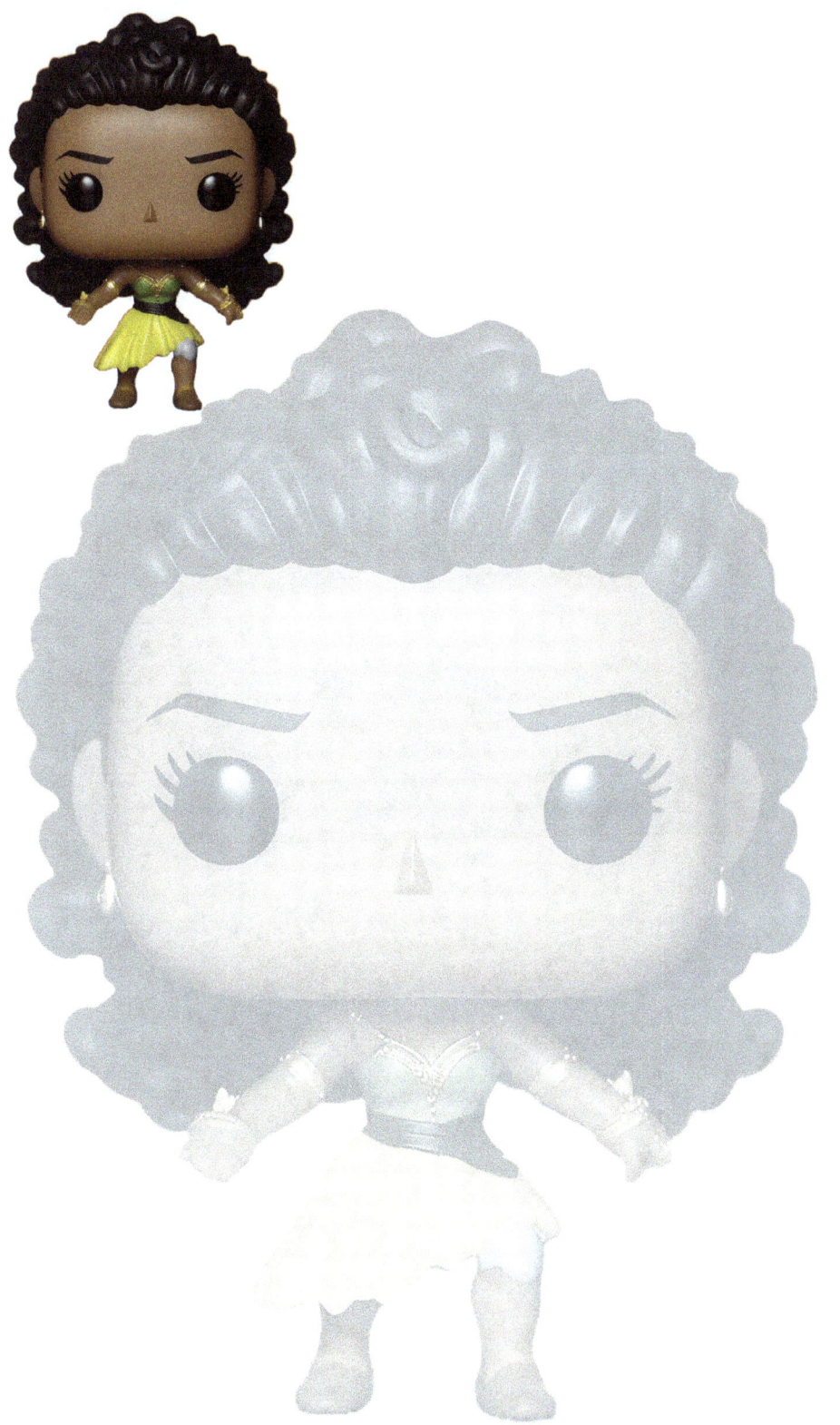

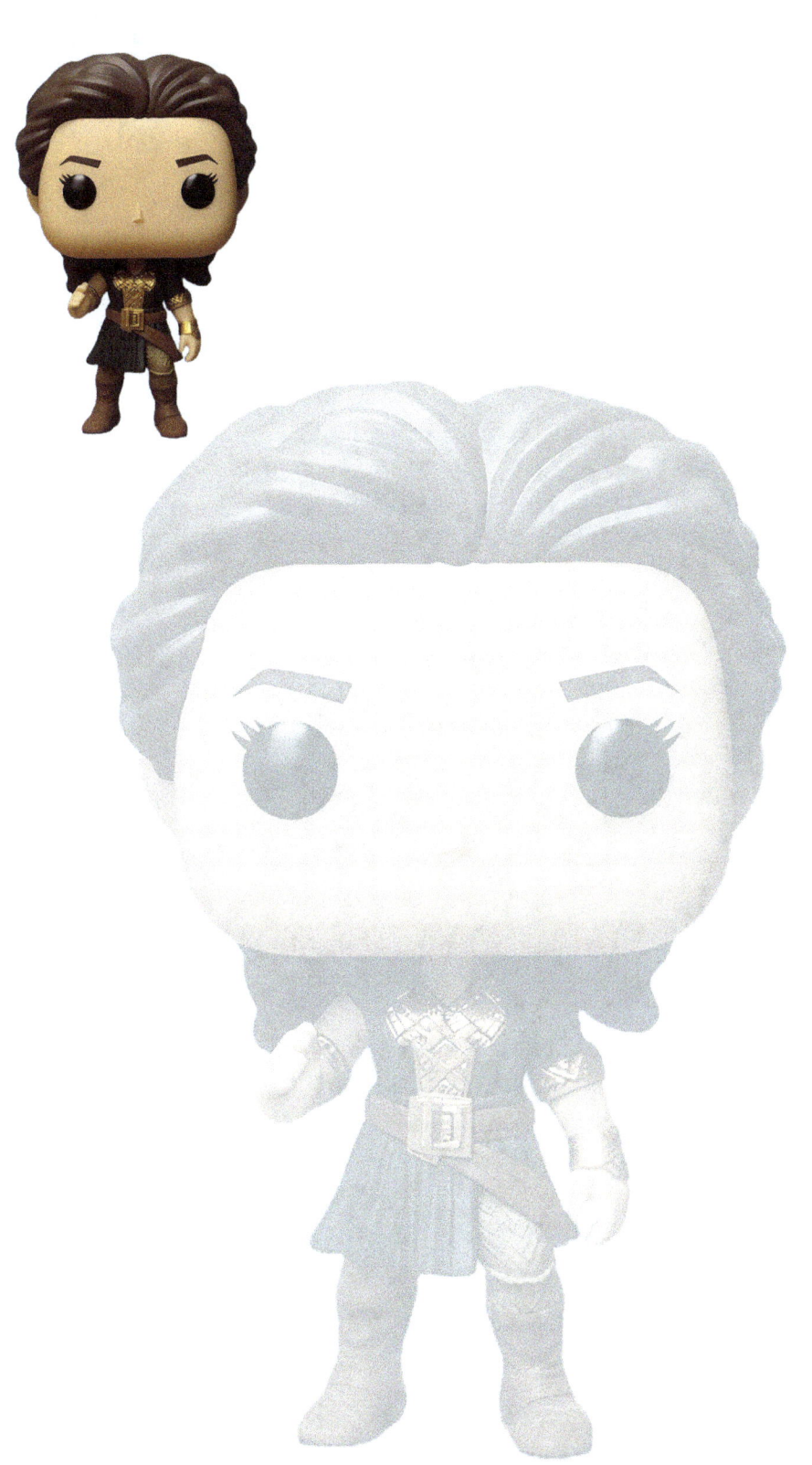

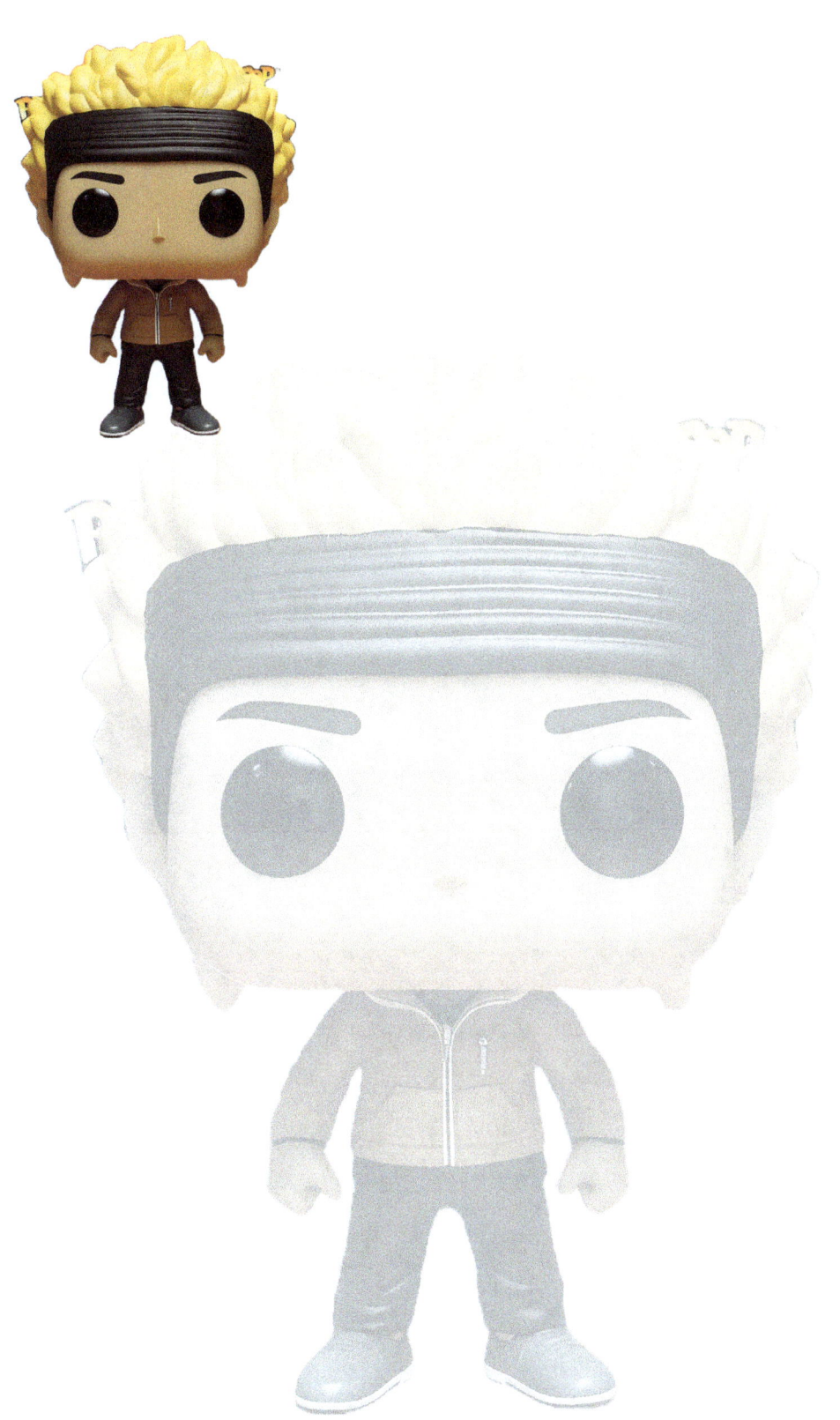

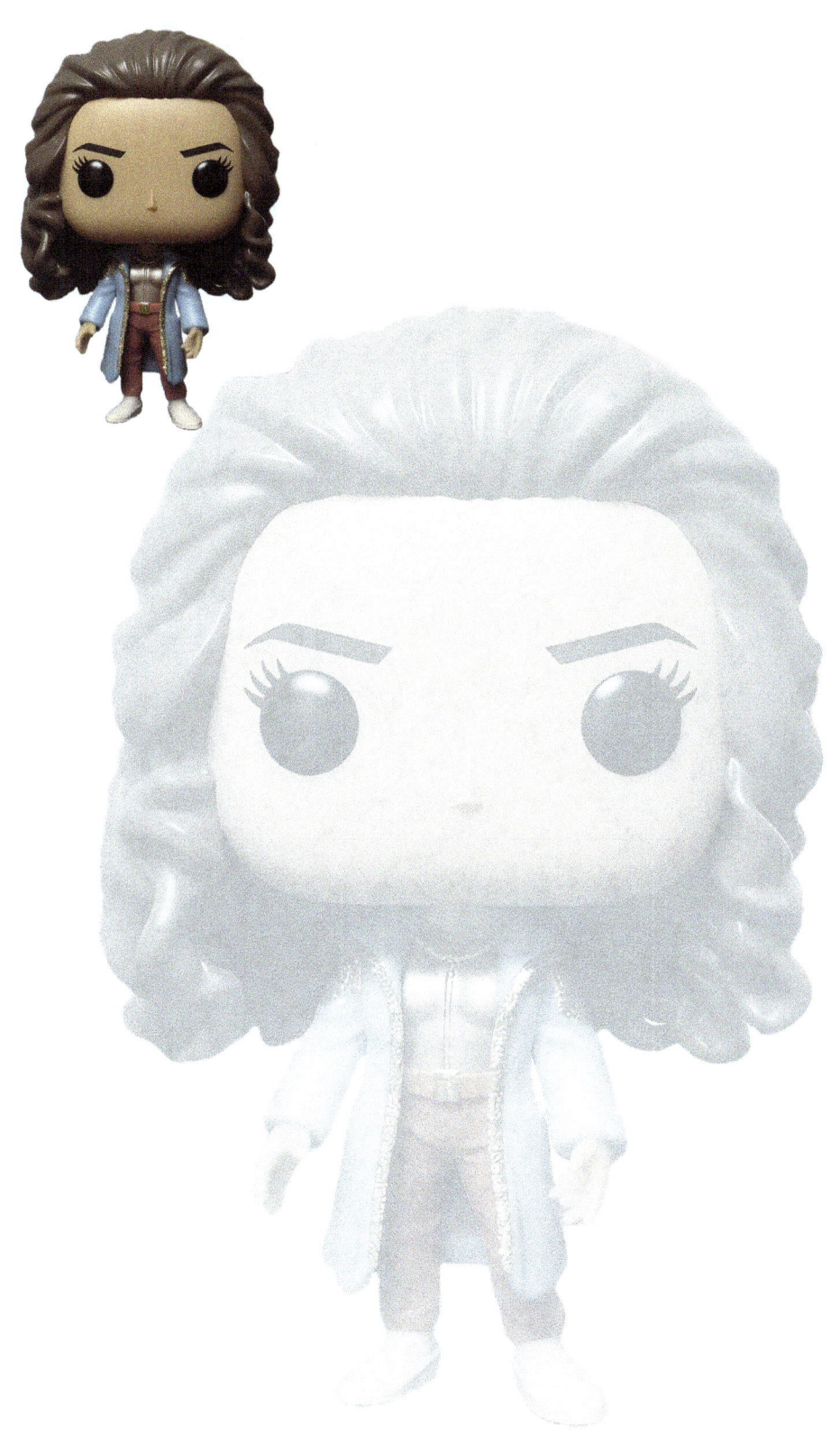

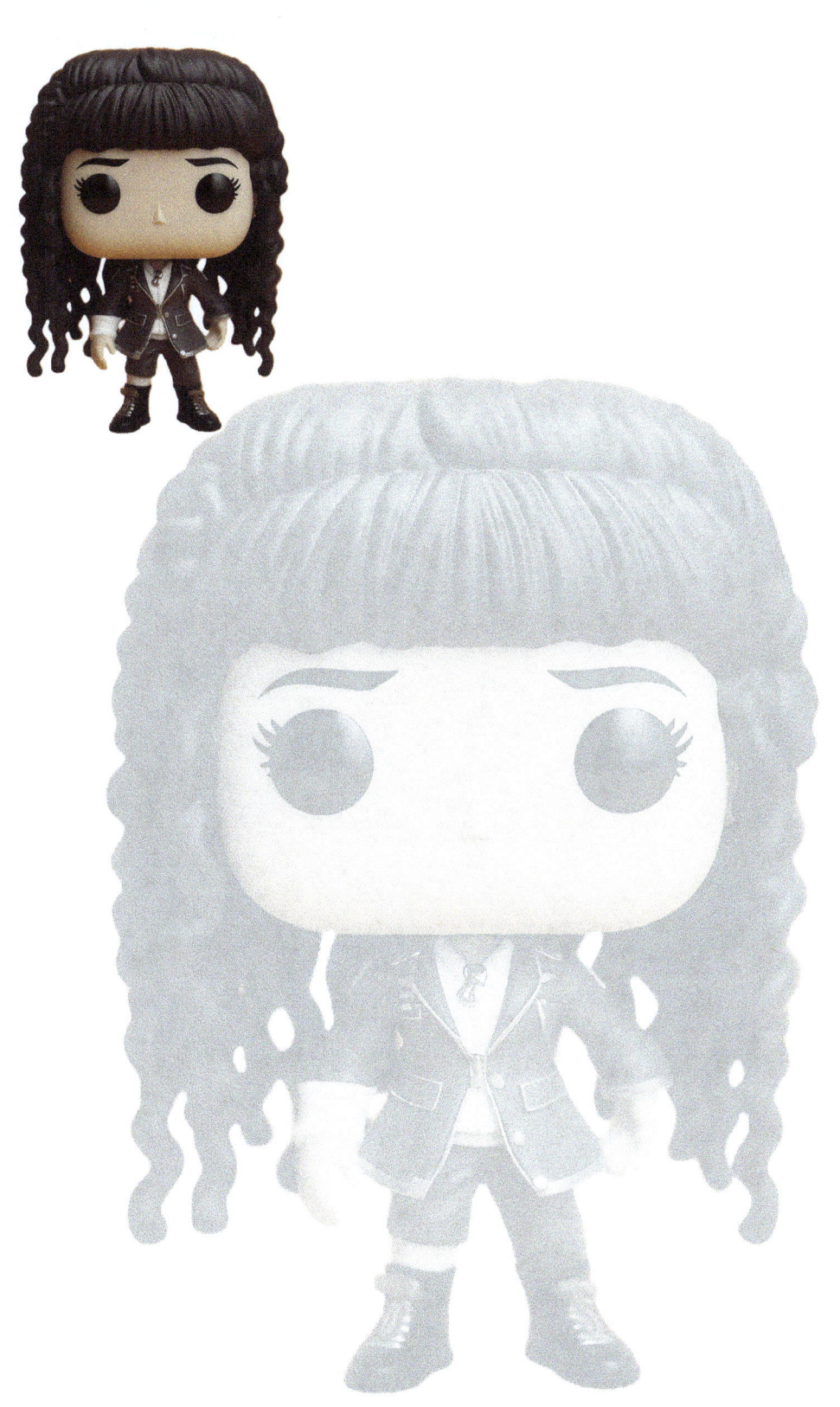

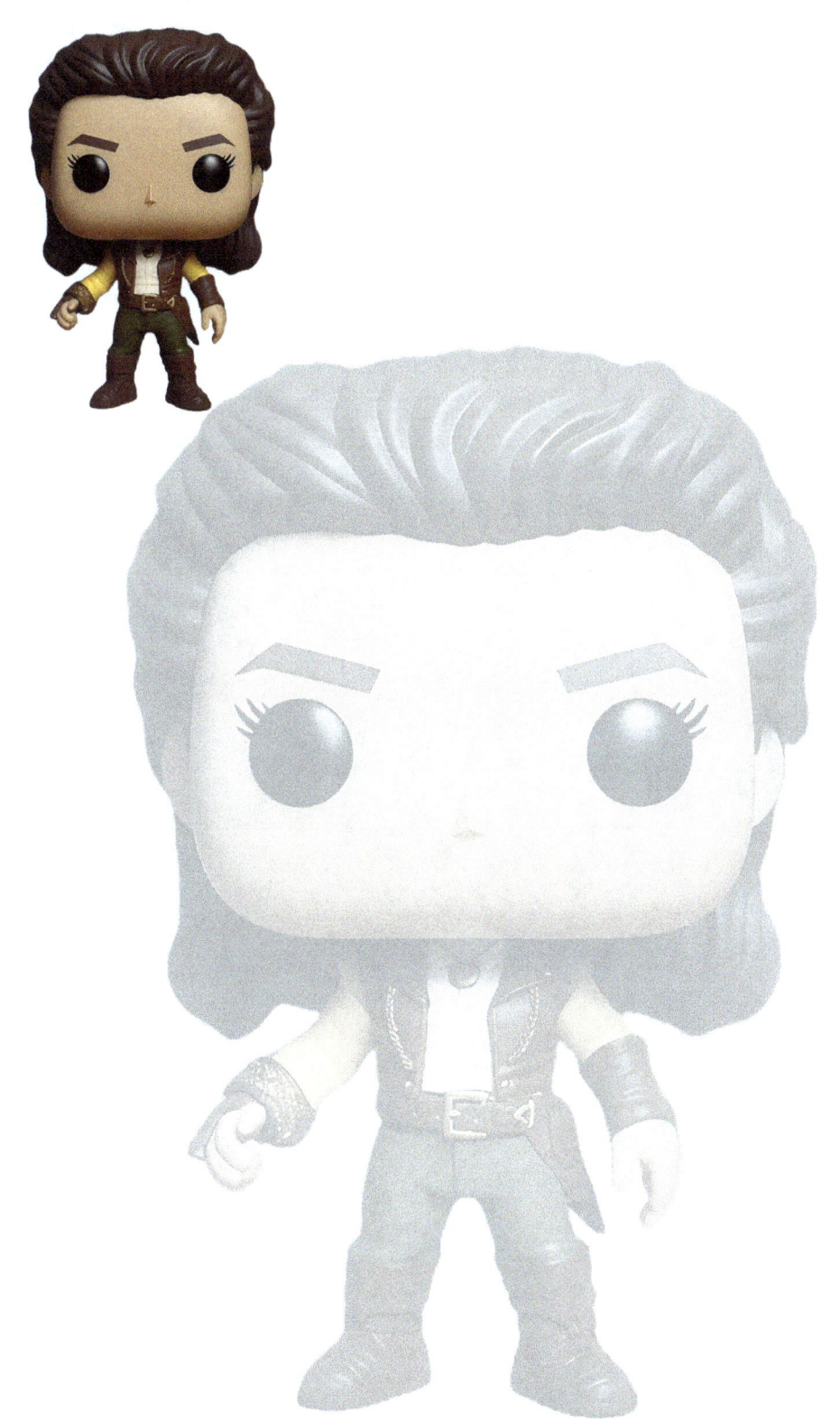

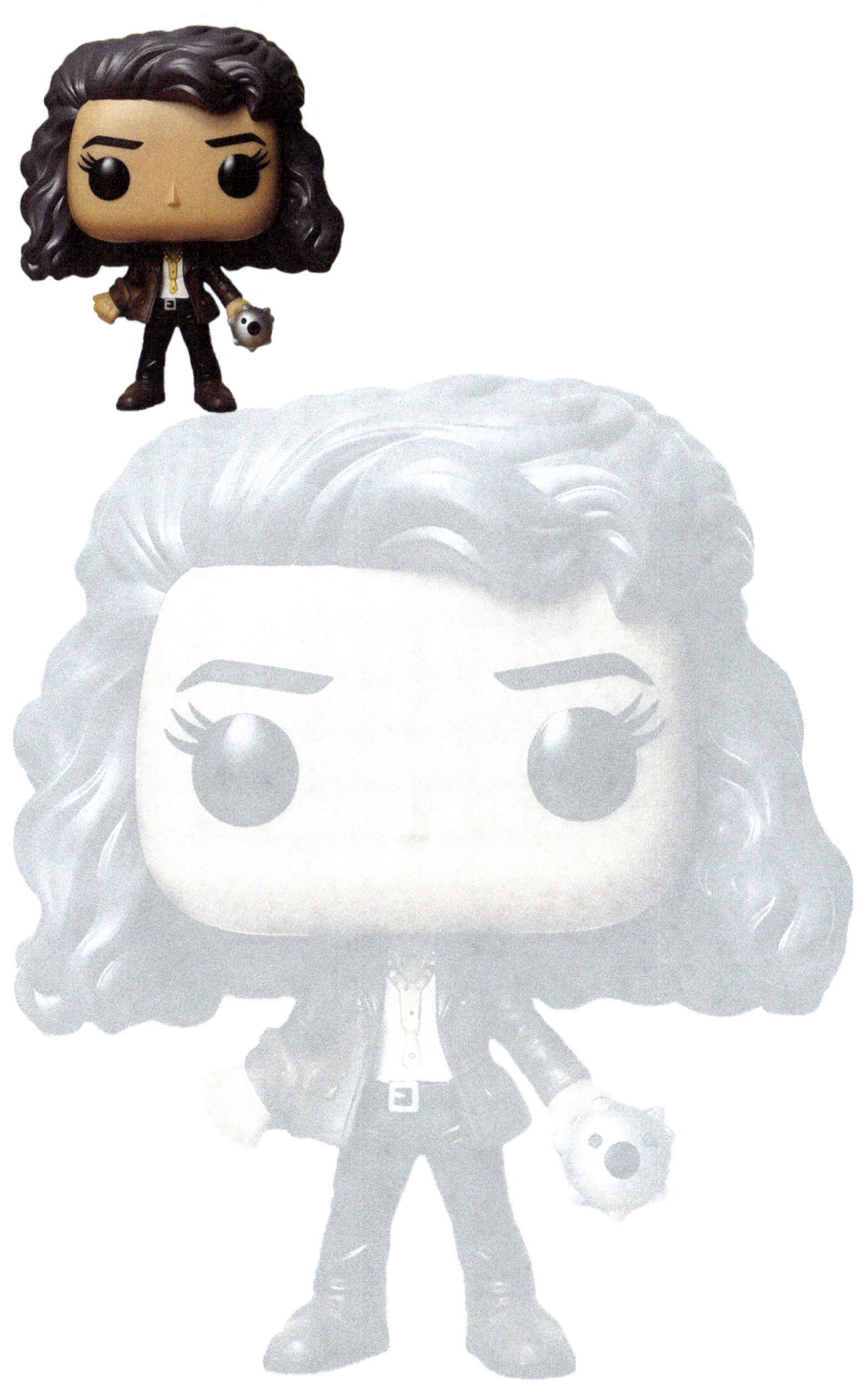

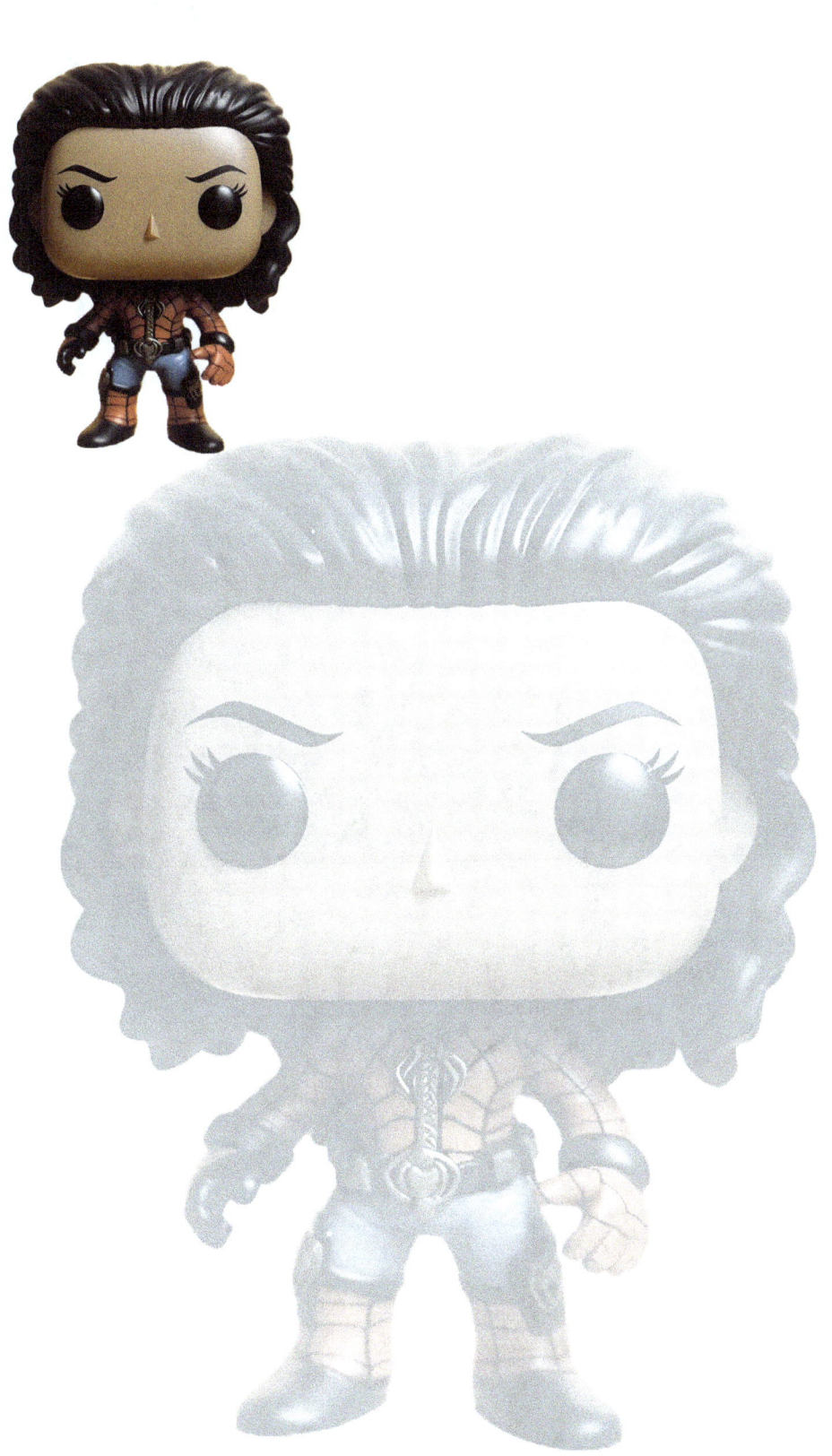

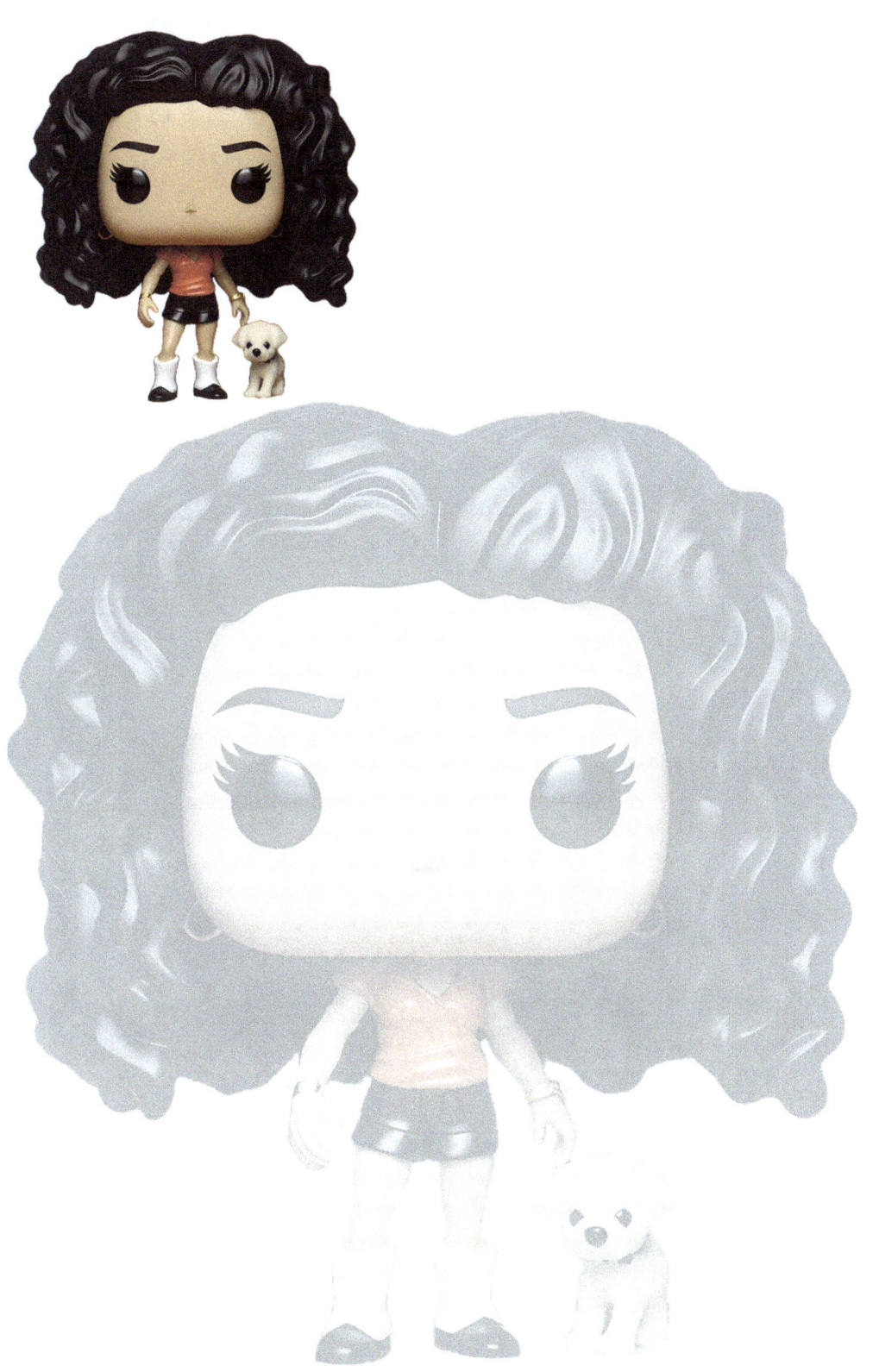

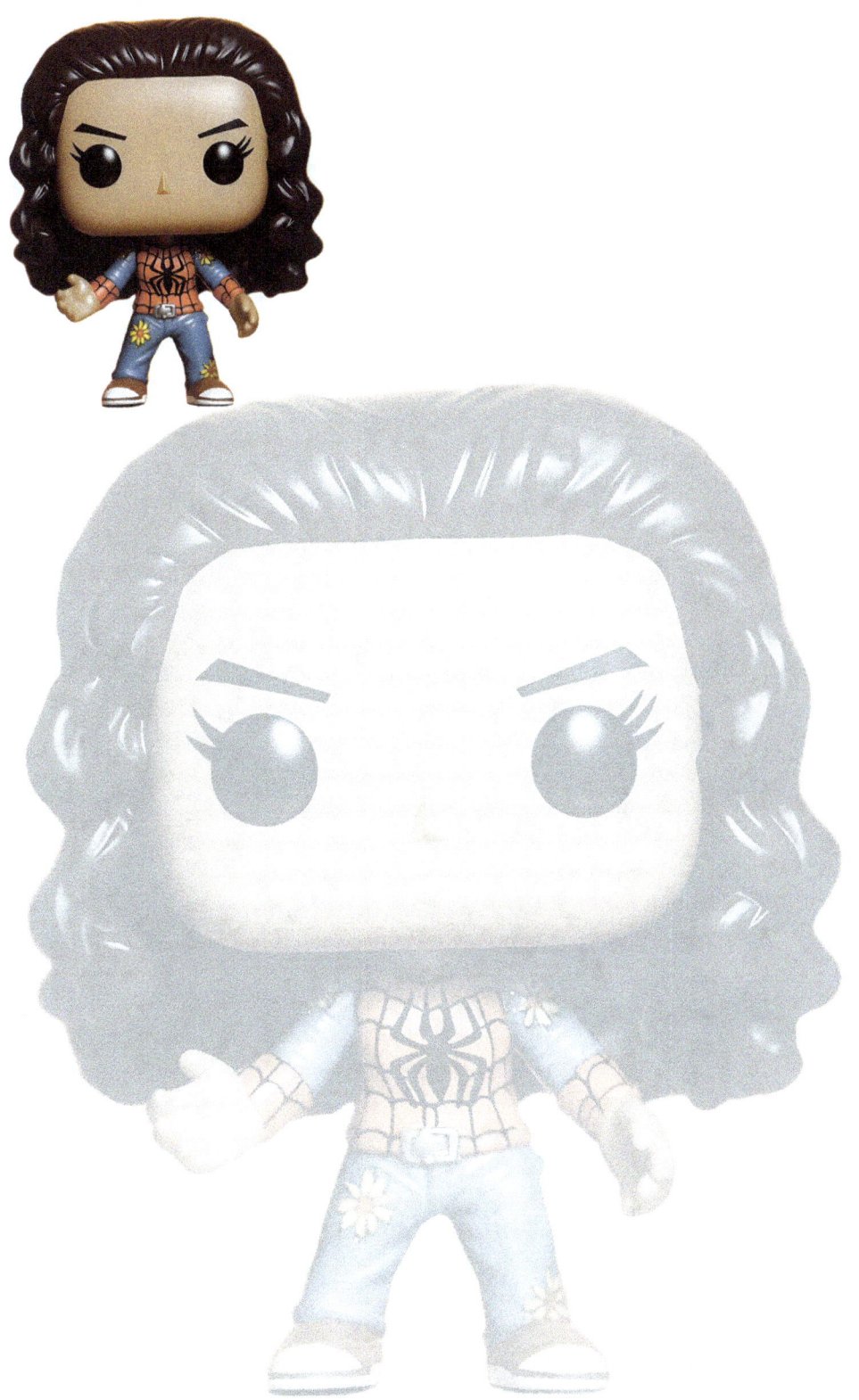

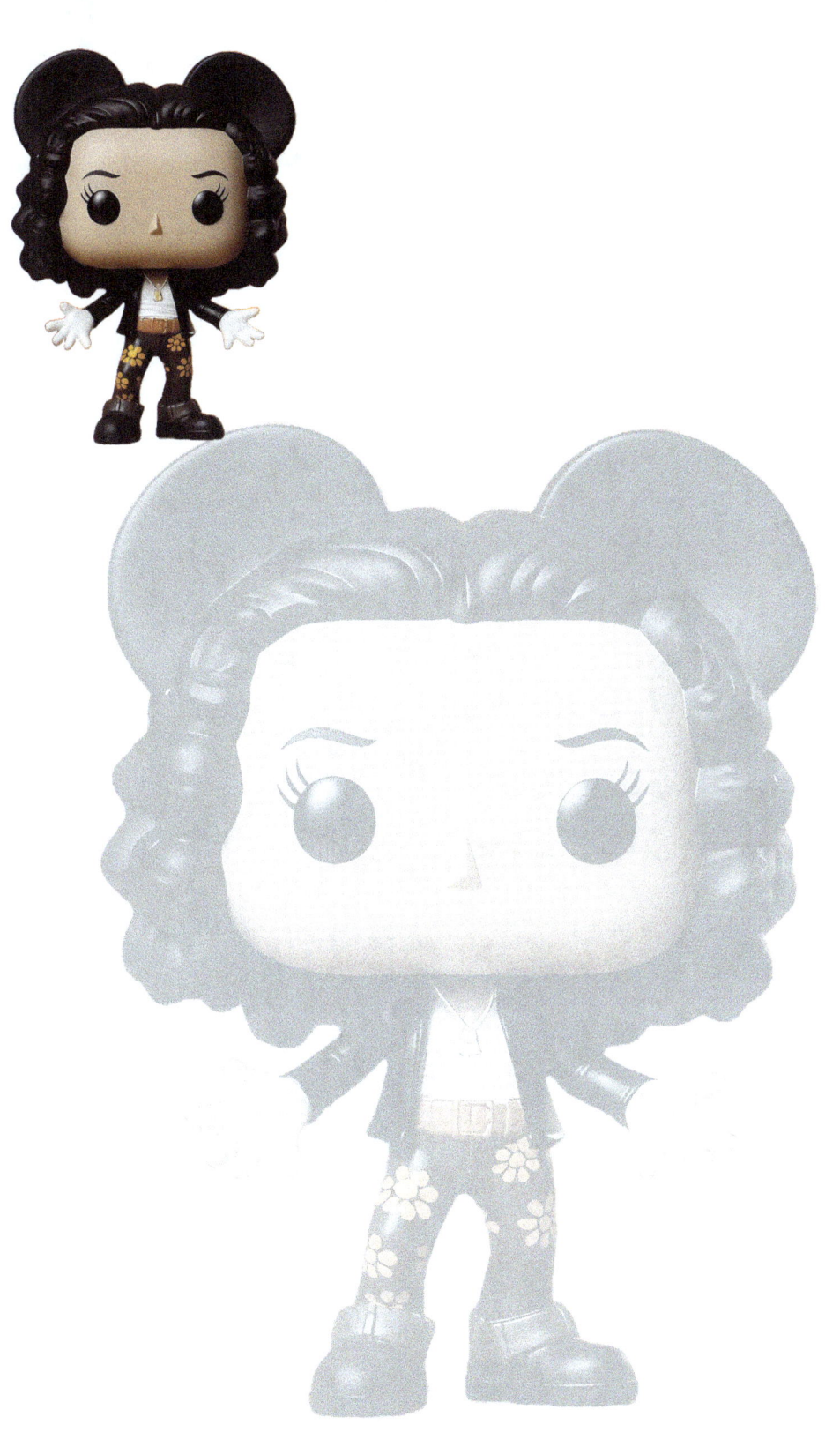

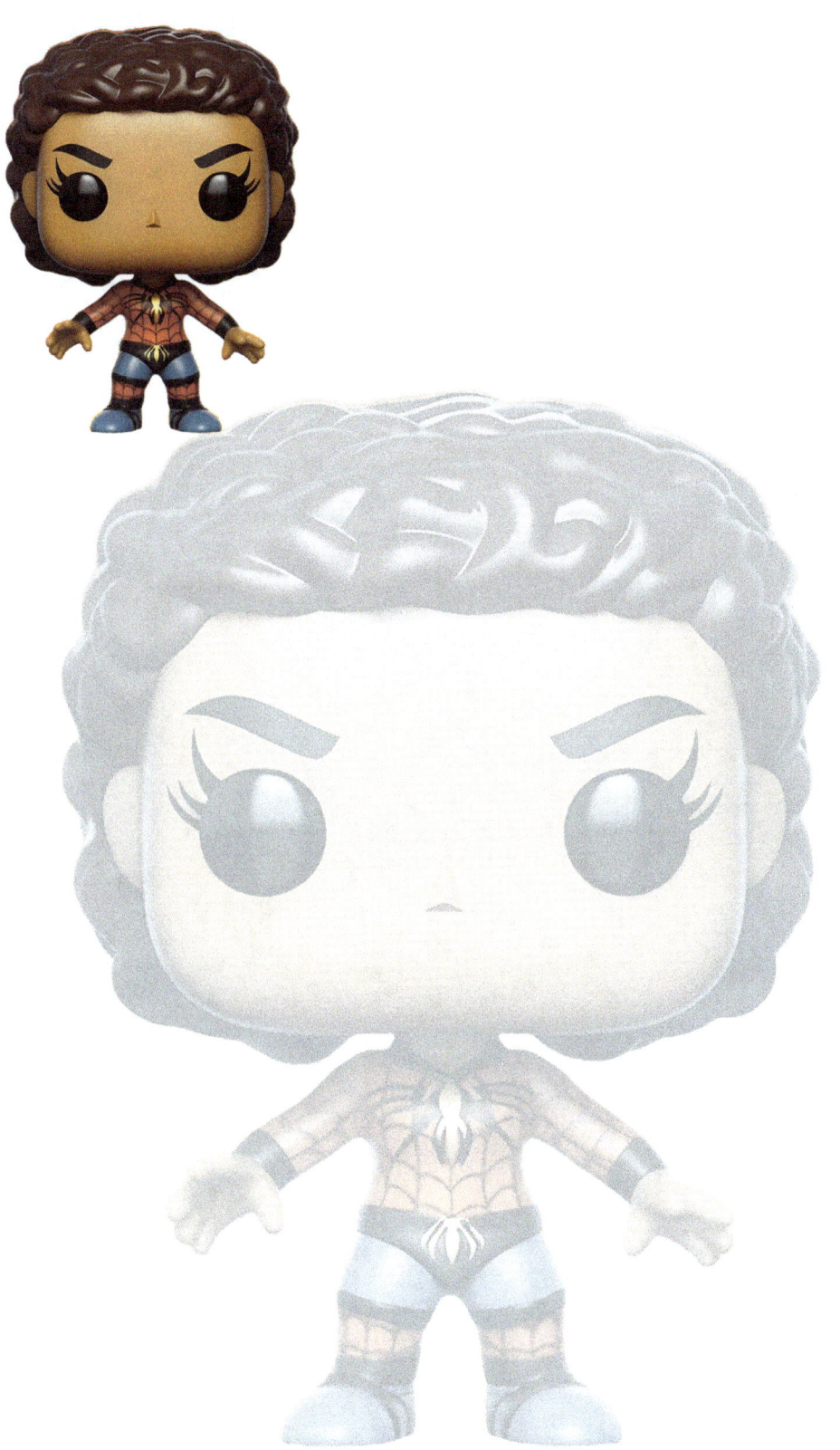

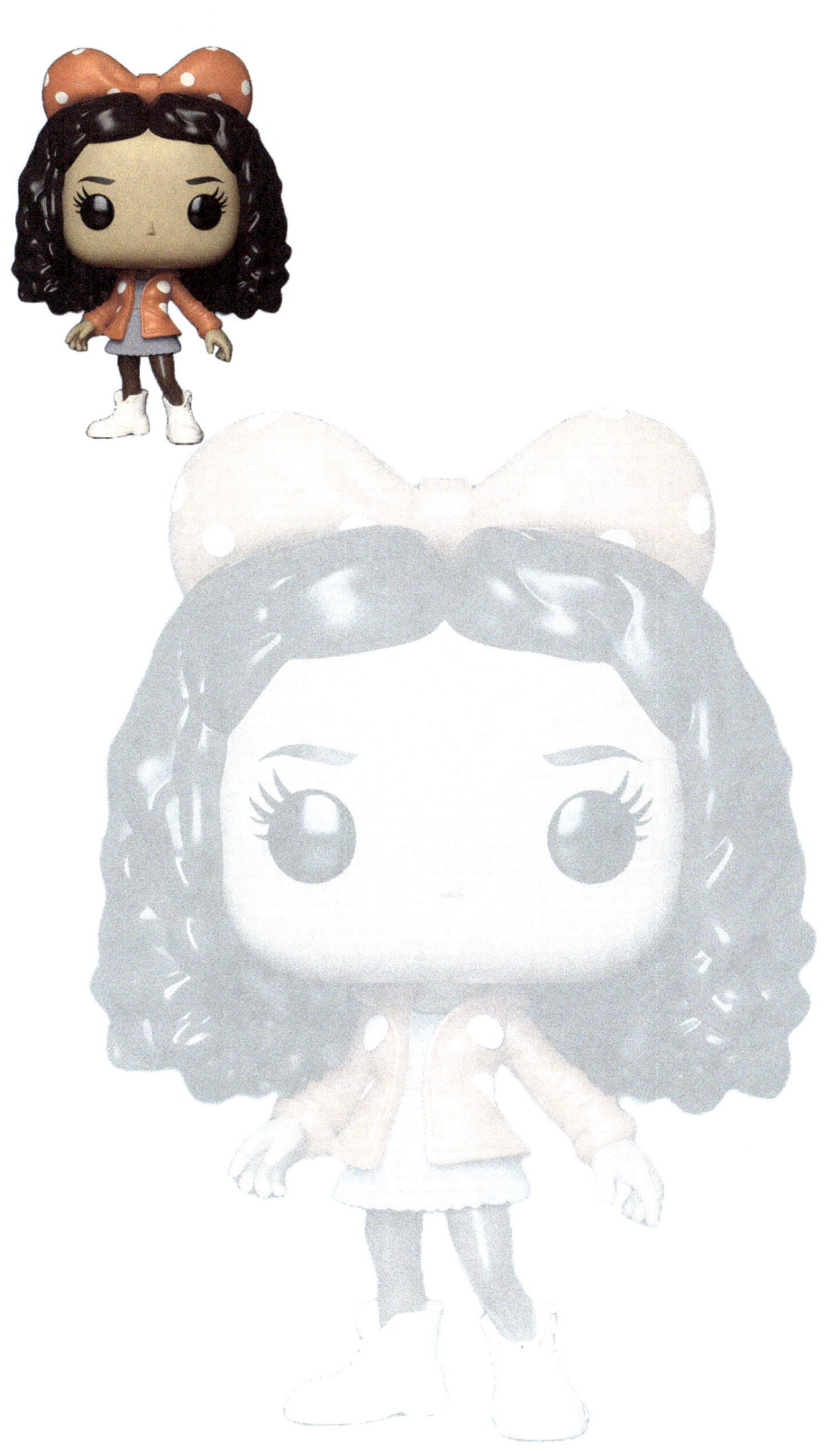

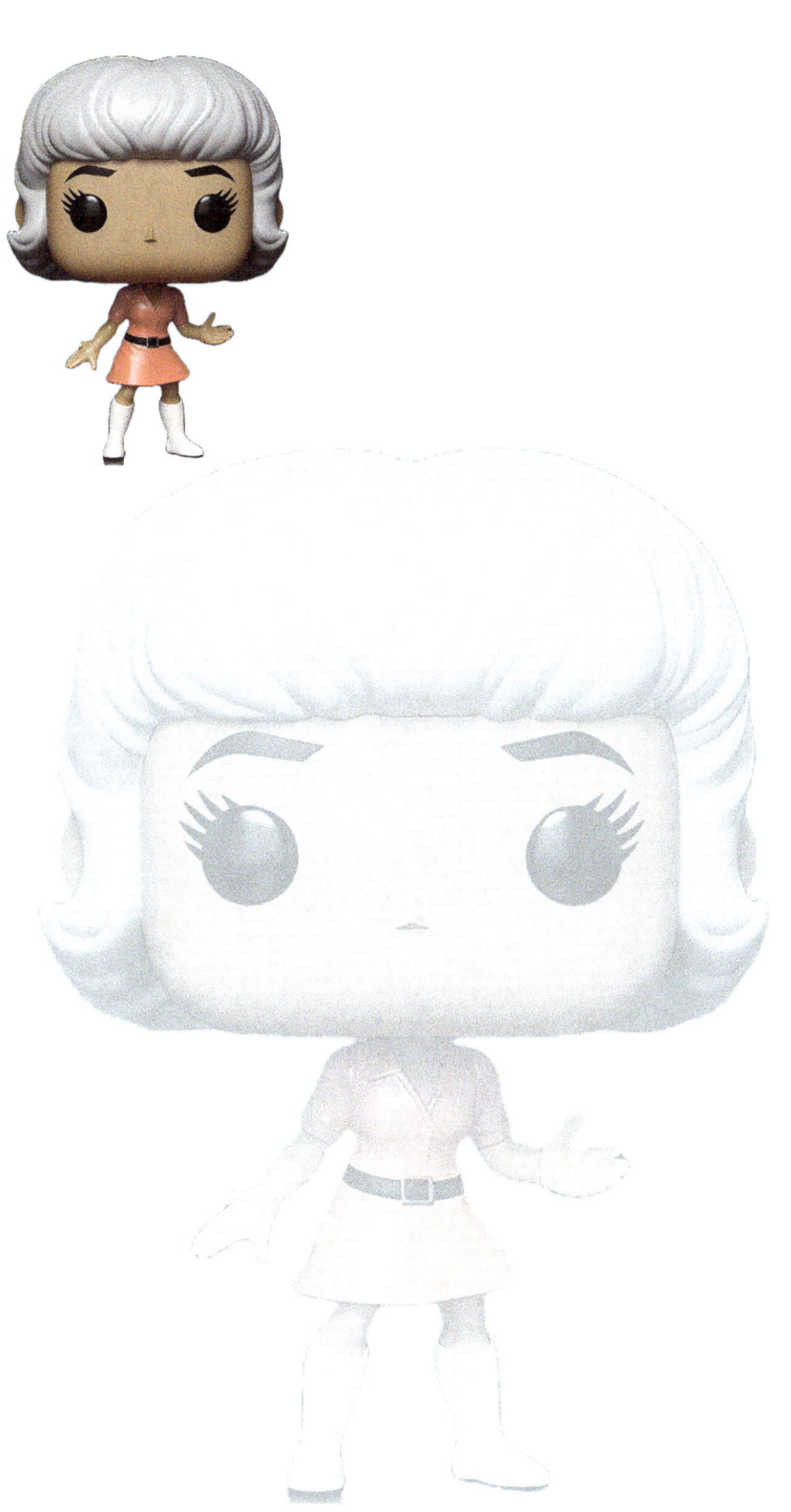

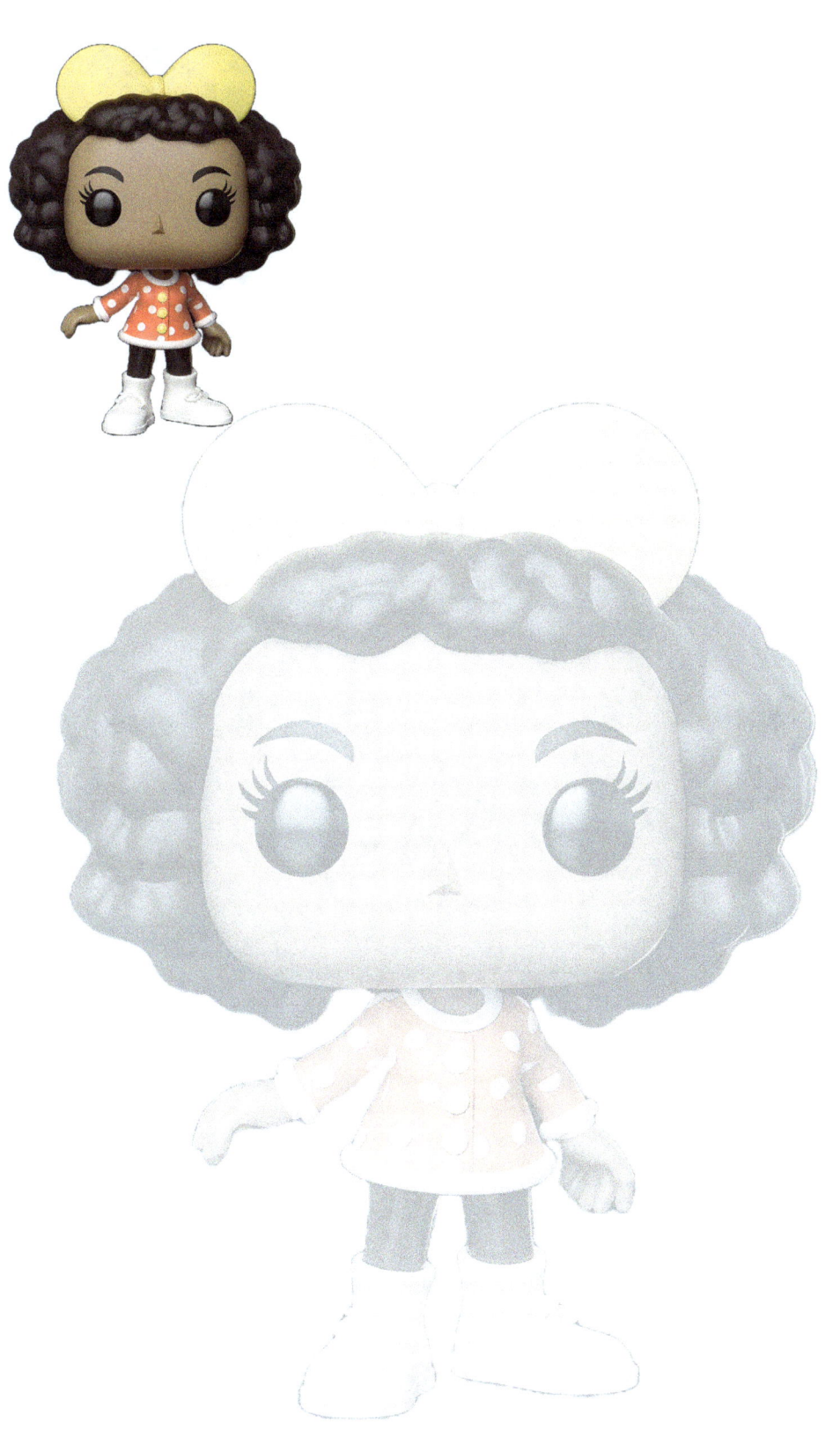